SRA Open Court Reading

Skills Practice

Blackline Masters with Answer Key

Grade 2

MHEonline.com

Copyright © 2016 McGraw-Hill Education

All rights reserved. The contents, or parts thereof, may be reproduced in print form for non-profit educational use with SRA Open Court Reading, provided such reproductions bear copyright notice, but may not be reproduced in any form for any other purpose without the prior written consent of McGraw-Hill Education, including, but not limited to, network storage or transmission, or broadcast for distance learning.

Send all inquiries to:
McGraw-Hill Education
8787 Orion Place
Columbus, OH 43240

ISBN: 978-0-02-145969-4
MHID: 0-02-145969-7

Printed in the United States of America

McGraw Hill Education

MHEonline.com

Mc
Graw
Hill
Education

Copyright © 2016 McGraw-Hill Education

All rights reserved. The contents, or parts thereof, may
be reproduced in print form for non-profit educational
use with *SRA Open Court Reading,* provided such
reproductions bear copyright notice, but may not be
reproduced in any form for any other purpose without
the prior written consent of McGraw-Hill Education,
including, but not limited to, network storage or
transmission, or broadcast for distance learning.

Send all inquiries to:
McGraw-Hill Education
8787 Orion Place
Columbus, OH 43240

ISBN: 978-0-02-145996-4
MHID: 0-02-145996-7

Printed in the United States of America

3 4 5 6 7 8 QVS 21 20 19 18 17

Table of Contents

Unit 3 My Community at Work

/ch/ spelled *ch*, /th/ spelled *th*, and /sh/ spelled *sh*

> **FOCUS** The letters in a consonant digraph combine to make one new sound. Some examples of consonant digraphs are /ch/ spelled *ch*, /th/ spelled *th*, and /sh/ spelled *sh*.

PRACTICE Sort the words below.
Write each word under the correct heading.

rash	thump	chap	pinch	shot
fish	with	chat	thorn	

/ch/	/th/	/sh/
1. _____	4. _____	7. _____
2. _____	5. _____	8. _____
3. _____	6. _____	9. _____

Copyright © McGraw-Hill Education. Permission is granted to reproduce for classroom use.

APPLY Choose a word from the box below to complete each sentence. Write the word on the line.

trash	chest	ship	thud	inch	moth	shed

10. A _____ docked in the harbor.

11. The _____ flaps its wings.

12. Sheldon fell to the floor with a _____.

13. Put all _____ in the black bin.

14. Samantha pinned a ribbon on her _____.

15. The pants are one _____ too short.

16. Our tools are in the _____.

Circle the word with /ch/ spelled _ch_, /th/ spelled _th_, or /sh/ spelled _sh_. Write the word on the line.

17. Mindy is a tennis champ. _____

18. The snow melted to slush. _____

19. Pack a lunch for the trip. _____

20. Ken will go with Skip. _____

Copyright © McGraw-Hill Education. Permission is granted to reproduce for classroom use.

/w/ spelled w*h*_ and /ar/ spelled *ar*

FOCUS
- The /w/ sound can be spelled *wh*_. A vowel always follows *wh* in this spelling of /w/.
- When the letter *r* follows a vowel, it often changes the vowel sound. When *r* follows the letter *a*, it usually makes the /ar/ sound.

PRACTICE Write the word from the box that best completes each sentence.

market	scarf	whip	when	dark	which

1. Grab a hat and a _____ before you go outside.

2. To _____ park should we go?

3. Come home before it gets _____.

4. Use a mixer to _____ the batter.

5. Get up _____ the alarm rings.

6. Carla got apples at the farmers' _____.

Copyright © McGraw-Hill Education. Permission is granted to reproduce for classroom use.

APPLY Use the letters in parentheses to make a word with /w/ spelled *wh_*.

7. (r, e, e) _____

8. (a, m) _____

9. (f, i, f) _____

10. (t, a) _____

Use the letters in parentheses to make a word with /ar/ spelled *ar*.

11. (d, t) _____

12. (p, s, k) _____

13. (g, d, n, e) _____

14. (h, c, m) _____

15. (n, b) _____

16. (s, p, h) _____

17. (d, h) _____

18. (y, n) _____

19. (s, t, t) _____

20. (a, r, d) _____

Copyright © McGraw-Hill Education. Permission is granted to reproduce for classroom use.

Vocabulary

> ## FOCUS
> Review the vocabulary words from "The Mice Who Lived in a Shoe."

admired	gathered	merchant	platform	shelter
fetched	huddled	observed	safety	timber

PRACTICE Circle the word in parentheses that best fits each sentence.

1. The birdwatcher (observed, huddled) a mother robin in a tree.

2. The robin had laid her eggs in the (safety, platform) of her nest.

3. The mother robin's warm feathers provided (shelter, timber) for the eggs.

4. The birdwatcher (admired, gathered) the way the mother cared for her eggs.

5. Using a camera he bought from a (merchant, shelter), the birdwatcher took pictures of the nest.

6. The birdwatcher noticed a raised (platform, huddle) next to the mother robin's nest.

7. He crept toward the structure and quietly climbed the (timber, safety) ladder.

8. Then he (huddled, sheltered) down and took several more lovely photographs of the mother robin.

Copyright © McGraw-Hill Education. Permission is granted to reproduce for classroom use.

Vocabulary

APPLY Read the definitions and the sentences.
Write the letter of the meaning that shows how the
underlined word is used in each sentence.

fetch

> **a.** to go after and bring back
>
> **b.** to get a certain price when something is sold

9. _____ I think my painting will <u>fetch</u> $100 dollars.

gather

> **a.** to come together
>
> **b.** a part of a piece of clothing that is drawn together

10. _____ The <u>gather</u> on her skirt was broken and
needed to be resewn.

Copyright © McGraw-Hill Education. Permission is granted to reproduce for classroom use.

Cause and Effect

> **FOCUS**
> - A **cause** is *why* something happens.
> - An **effect** is *what* happens.

PRACTICE Read each sentence. Write the *effect* (what happened) and the *cause* (why it happened).

1. Because the shoe had holes in it, the mice needed a new home.

   Effect: _____

   Cause: _____

2. Pa sold their broken furniture, so then he had money to buy some tools.

   Effect: _____

   Cause: _____

3. Because the new house had a roof, the family stayed dry.

   Effect: _____

   Cause: _____

Copyright © McGraw-Hill Education. Permission is granted to reproduce for classroom use.

Cause and Effect

APPLY Read each effect below. Write a cause to complete each sentence.

4. The lamp broke because _____.

5. Nick's face was sunburned because _____.

6. The pitcher was empty because _____.

Look at "The Mice Who Lived in a Shoe" for the effects listed below. Then write the cause for each one.

7. **Effect:** The family huddled together and squeaked.

   Cause: _____

8. **Effect:** The cat could not stretch his claws in the shoe.

   Cause: _____

Copyright © McGraw-Hill Education. Permission is granted to reproduce for classroom use.

Access Complex Text • *Skills Practice 1*

Writing an Opinion Piece

Think

Audience: *Who* will read your opinion?

_____

_____

Purpose: *What* is your reason for writing about your opinion?

_____

_____

Prewriting

Brainstorm ideas for writing your opinion piece.

1. _____

2. _____

3. _____

4. _____

5. _____

6. _____

Copyright © McGraw-Hill Education. Permission is granted to reproduce for classroom use.

Revising

Use this checklist to revise your opinion piece.

- ☐ Does your writing state an opinion?

- ☐ Does your writing have reasons that support your opinion?

- ☐ Does your writing include interesting details or descriptions?

- ☐ Did you include an ending that sums up your opinion?

- ☐ Does your writing include linking words?

Editing/Proofreading

Use this checklist to correct mistakes in your opinion piece.

- ☐ Did you use proofreading symbols when editing?

- ☐ Did you capitalize the first word of each sentence and all proper nouns?

- ☐ Did you check your writing for spelling mistakes?

Publishing

Use this checklist to prepare your opinion piece for publishing.

- ☐ Write or type a neat copy of your opinion piece.

- ☐ Add a photograph or a drawing.

Copyright © McGraw-Hill Education. Permission is granted to reproduce for classroom use.

/ch/ spelled *ch*; /th/ spelled *th*; /sh/ spelled *sh*; /w/ spelled *wh_*; /ar/ spelled *ar*

FOCUS
- One way the /ch/ sound can be spelled is *ch*.
- One way the /th/ sound can be spelled is *th*.
- One way the /sh/ sound can be spelled is *sh*.
- One way the /w/ sound can be spelled is *wh_*.
- One way the /ar/ sound can be spelled is *ar*.

PRACTICE Sort the spelling words. Some words will appear under more than one heading.

/ch/ spelled *ch*

1. _____
2. _____
3. _____
4. _____

/th/ spelled *th*

12. _____
13. _____

/sh/ spelled *sh*

5. _____
6. _____
7. _____
8. _____

/w/ spelled *wh_*

14. _____

/ar/ spelled *ar*

9. _____
10. _____
11. _____

Word List		**Challenge Words**
1. ship	**6.** shed	**11.** what
2. chin	**7.** with	**12.** chef
3. that	**8.** shark	**13.** when
4. march	**9.** chop	**14.** shoe
5. which	**10.** harsh	**15.** throw

Copyright © McGraw-Hill Education. Permission is granted to reproduce for classroom use.

APPLY Replace the underlined letter or letters to create a spelling word.

15. <u>b</u>ark + sh = _____

16. <u>m</u>arsh + h = _____

17. <u>fl</u>at + th = _____

18. <u>thin</u> + ch = _____

19. <u>ch</u>ip + sh = _____

20. <u>cr</u>op + ch = _____

Circle the correct spelling for each spelling word.
Write the correct spelling on the line.

21. with   whith   _____

22. wich   which   _____

23. shed   sched   _____

24. marsch   march   _____

Copyright © McGraw-Hill Education. Permission is granted to reproduce for classroom use.

Name _____ **Date** _____

Common and Proper Nouns

> ***FOCUS***
> - A **common noun** names a person, a place, a thing, or an idea. A common noun does not begin with a capital letter.
>   **Examples:** dancer, country car, color, happiness
> - A **proper noun** names a *certain* person, place, or thing. A proper noun begins with a capital letter.
>   **Examples:** Dr. Green, America, English

PRACTICE Underline the *proper noun* or *nouns* in each sentence.

1. Mrs. Smith has a new baby girl.

2. The baby's name is Allison.

3. We went to see the baby at Riverside Hospital.

Underline the *common noun* or *nouns* in each sentence.

4. My class is reading about fish.

5. We must do kind things.

6. I helped Mrs. Jones find her glasses.

Copyright © McGraw-Hill Education. Permission is granted to reproduce for classroom use.

APPLY Read the paragraph below. Underline with three lines the letters of proper nouns that need to be capitalized. Circle the common nouns.

My name is melissa. I am a student at goshen lane elementary school. Right now, I am in the second grade, and mr. sanchez is my teacher. My best friend, hilary, has a different teacher. We get to play together at recess. Every tuesday afternoon we have a music class together. School is a great place to learn new things and make great friends.

Read the common noun listed, and write a proper noun to tell about yourself. Make sure to begin each proper noun with a capital letter.

Common Noun	Proper Noun
7. name	_____
8. where you live	_____
9. school	_____
10. teacher	_____

Copyright © McGraw-Hill Education. Permission is granted to reproduce for classroom use.

Closed Syllables

> ***FOCUS***
> - A closed syllable occurs when a vowel spelling is followed by a consonant spelling. The vowel sound is usually short.
> - If a word has two consonant spellings in the middle, you usually divide the word between the two consonants.

PRACTICE **Look at how the syllables are divided in the words below. Circle the correct way to divide each word.**

1. pep/per   pe/pper

2. pic/nic   pi/cnic

3. exp/and   ex/pand

4. hic/cup   hicc/up

5. shelt/er   shel/ter

6. tu/nnel   tun/nel

7. ta/blet   tab/let

8. cob/web   co/bweb

9. bask/et   bas/ket

Copyright © McGraw-Hill Education. Permission is granted to reproduce for classroom use.

APPLY Divide each word into syllables.

10. mantel _____

11. rabbit _____

12. laptop _____

13. classic _____

14. temper _____

15. slipper _____

Use the words above to write five different sentences.

16. _____

_____

17. _____

_____

18. _____

_____

19. _____

_____

20. _____

_____

Copyright © McGraw-Hill Education. Permission is granted to reproduce for classroom use.

/j/ spelled ■*dge*, /k/ spelled ■*ck*, and /ch/ spelled ■*tch*

FOCUS
- The /j/ sound can be spelled ■*dge*. A short-vowel sound comes before this spelling.
- The /k/ sound can be spelled ■*ck*. A short-vowel sound comes before this spelling.
- The /ch/ sound can be spelled ■*tch*. A short-vowel sound comes before this spelling.

PRACTICE Circle the spelling for /j/, /k/, or /ch/. Then write the short-vowel spelling for each word.

1. patch _____

2. crack _____

3. tickle _____

4. ridge _____

5. batch _____

6. pledge _____

Copyright © McGraw-Hill Education. Permission is granted to reproduce for classroom use.

APPLY Read the words in the box. Write *dge*, *ck*, or *tch* in each space to spell one of the words.

nudge	locker	stretch	pitcher	track	bridge

7. stre_____

8. lo_____er

9. bri_____

10. pi_____er

11. nu_____

12. tra_____

Use a word from above to complete each sentence.

13. The pups _____ and sniff each other.

14. The _____ is full of milk.

15. Put your jacket in the _____.

16. Fast cars zip around the _____.

17. We bend and _____ before we run.

18. A _____ spans the big river.

Copyright © McGraw-Hill Education. Permission is granted to reproduce for classroom use.

Vocabulary

> **FOCUS** Review the vocabulary words from "Ants and Aphids Work Together."

colony	liquid	predators	scurry	symbiosis
honeydew	partners	relationship	shelter	team

PRACTICE Circle Yes or No to answer each question below.

1. Can a *team* play a game?

Yes   No

2. If an insect kills a plant, is that an example of *symbiosis*?

Yes   No

3. Do good *partners* work together well?

Yes   No

4. Is there a *relationship* between parents and children?

Yes   No

5. Do animals in a *colony* live alone?

Yes   No

Copyright © McGraw-Hill Education. Permission is granted to reproduce for classroom use.

Vocabulary

APPLY Use a vocabulary word to answer each riddle below.

6. A house, an umbrella, and a tent are all kinds of this:

_____

7. I am not ice. I am not a gas. I flow down, not up. What am I?

_____

8. Lions, tigers, and bears are all examples of these:

_____

9. One insect makes me. Another insect eats me. I am sweet. What am I?

_____

10. I am another word for *run in a hurry*. What word am I?

_____

Copyright © McGraw-Hill Education. Permission is granted to reproduce for classroom use.

Compare and Contrast

> **FOCUS**
> - To *compare* means to tell how things, events, or characters are alike. Some comparison clue words are *both, same, like,* and *too.*
> - To *contrast* means to tell how things, events, or characters are different. Some contrast clue words are *different, but,* and *unlike.*

PRACTICE Circle whether the sentence is *comparing* or *contrasting*. Then write the clue word on the line.

1. Aphids hurt plants, but ladybugs do not.

    compare   contrast   _____

2. Ants and aphids are both types of insects.

    compare   contrast   _____

3. Insects and spiders have different numbers of legs.

    compare   contrast   _____

4. Unlike ants, aphids do not fight predators.

    compare   contrast   _____

Copyright © McGraw-Hill Education. Permission is granted to reproduce for classroom use.

Compare and Contrast

APPLY Look again at "Ants and Aphids Work Together." Then read the following text about scales.

Scales are tiny insects. They suck juices from trees and bushes. Scales turn those juices into honeydew. Unlike aphids, scales do not suck juices from vegetable plants. Scales stay in the same place for most of their lives. They do not look like other insects.

Now compare and contrast scales and aphids. Write one sentence telling how they are alike. Then write one sentence telling how they are different.

5. Compare (same):

_____

_____

_____

6. Contrast (different):

_____

_____

_____

Copyright © McGraw-Hill Education. Permission is granted to reproduce for classroom use.

Writing an Opinion Piece

Think

Audience: *Who* will read your opinion?

_____

Purpose: *What* is your reason for writing about your opinion?

_____

Prewriting

Add interesting details and descriptions.

1. Reason #1: _____

Explanation #1: _____

Additional Detail: _____

2. Reason #2: _____

Explanation #2: _____

Additional Detail: _____

3. Reason #3: _____

Explanation #3: _____

Additional Detail: _____

Copyright © McGraw-Hill Education. Permission is granted to reproduce for classroom use.

Proofreading Symbols

¶   Indent the paragraph.

^   Add something.

ℓ   Take out something.

/   Make a small letter.

≡   Make a capital letter.

sp   Check spelling.

⊙   Add a period.

Copyright © McGraw-Hill Education. Permission is granted to reproduce for classroom use.

Closed Syllables; /j/ spelled ■dge; /k/ spelled ■ck; /ch/ spelled ■tch

> **FOCUS**
> • Closed syllables end in a vowel followed by a consonant. The vowel sound is usually short. All the spelling words contain closed syllables.
> • One way /j/ can be spelled is ■dge.
> • One way /k/ can be spelled is ■ck.
> • One way /ch/ can be spelled is ■tch

PRACTICE Sort the spelling words under the correct heading. Words may appear under more than one heading

/j/ spelled ■dge

1. _____

2. _____

3. _____

4. _____

/k/ spelled ■ck

5. _____

6. _____

7. _____

8. _____

/ch/ spelled ■tch

9. _____

10. _____

Word List		Challenge Words
1. check	6. switch	11. catcher
2. wedge	7. track	12. watch
3. latch	8. ledge	13. locket
4. judge	9. badge	14. hatchet
5. kick	10. flock	15. fidget

Copyright © McGraw-Hill Education. Permission is granted to reproduce for classroom use.

APPLY Write the correct spelling word next to the appropriate clue.

11. something you can do to a football _____

12. a group of birds _____

13. a small, triangular shape _____

14. someone who makes decisions _____

15. to look carefully _____

Circle the correct spelling for each spelling word.
Write the correct spelling on the line.

16. swich   switch   _____

17. badge   badj   _____

18. track   trak   _____

19. latch   lach   _____

20. lej   ledge   _____

Copyright © McGraw-Hill Education. Permission is granted to reproduce for classroom use.

Action Verbs

FOCUS • An **action verb** tells what someone or something is doing.

Example: We *played* in the park for two hours.

PRACTICE Circle the action verb in each sentence.

1. Every Saturday, I play at the park.

2. I saw some broken swings and litter.

3. My family wanted to help.

4. Mom and Dad fixed the swings.

5. Grandma and I planted some flowers.

6. Then we all cleaned up the litter.

7. Everyone said the park was beautiful.

8. How can you make the world a better place?

Copyright © McGraw-Hill Education. Permission is granted to reproduce for classroom use.

APPLY Read the paragraph below. Write an action verb from the box in each blank.

pack	use	recycle	help	love
made	save	sort	putting	take

It is important for every person to
_____. You can _____
Earth and _____ energy. You can
_____ trash at home into paper,
plastic, and metal containers. New things can be
_____ from these used items. People
can also _____ things in different
ways instead of _____ them in the
trash. For example, _____ your lunch
in a reusable bag. You can also _____
a cloth bag to the grocery store. There are many ways to
_____ Earth.

Read the story below. Circle the best action verb for each sentence.

The first Earth Day **happened/are** in 1970. Every
year on April 22, people **do/find** things to **use/help**
Earth. We should **make/take** every day Earth Day.

Copyright © McGraw-Hill Education. Permission is granted to reproduce for classroom use.

Inflectional Endings -s and -es

> **FOCUS** Plural words show that there is more than one.
> Adding -s or -es to a noun makes it a regular plural.

PRACTICE Read each singular noun.
Then circle its plural form.

1. brush   brushs   brushes

2. box   boxs   boxes

3. wish   wishs   wishes

4. path   paths   pathes

5. class   classs   classes

6. chart   charts   chartes

7. champ   champs   champes

8. suffix   suffixs   suffixes

Copyright © McGraw-Hill Education. Permission is granted to reproduce for classroom use.

APPLY Read each singular noun in the box. Then write the plural form of the noun under the correct heading.

| fox | shark | branch | hill |

-s   **-es**

9. _____   11. _____

10. _____   12. _____

Write a sentence using each plural word from above.

13. _____

_____

14. _____

_____

15. _____

_____

16. _____

_____

Copyright © McGraw-Hill Education. Permission is granted to reproduce for classroom use.

Inflectional Ending -*ed*

FOCUS
- The inflectional ending -*ed* can be added to a base word. The meaning of the word is not changed. Only the form and function of the word changes.
- The -*ed* ending is used with the past tense form of a verb. It lets you know something has already happened.

PRACTICE Add -*ed* to each word.
Write the new word on the line.

1. dodge _____

2. blossom _____

3. stretch _____

4. plan _____

5. instruct _____

6. shrug _____

Copyright © McGraw-Hill Education. Permission is granted to reproduce for classroom use.

APPLY Circle the correct spelling for each word.
Write the correct spelling on the line.

7. tricked   trickd   _____

8. claped   clapped   _____

9. pledged   pledgeed   _____

10. expanded   expandd   _____

11. patched   patchd   _____

Use a word from above to complete each sentence.

12. Stan _____ that he would do the dishes.

13. Erin _____ her ripped jacket.

14. Martha _____ us and hid in the closet.

15. We _____ for the winners of the
tennis match.

16. The balloon _____ with air.

Copyright © McGraw-Hill Education. Permission is granted to reproduce for classroom use.

Vocabulary

> **FOCUS** Review the vocabulary words from "The Bat, Birds, and Beasts"

accepted	annual	emphasize	inquired	loyal	strategy

PRACTICE Circle the correct word that completes each sentence.

1. A farmer wanted to _____ that his sons should work together.

    a. inquired   **b.** emphasize   **c.** accepted

2. He had a good _____ to win the game.

    a. strategy   **b.** loyal   **c.** annual

3. He _____, "Can anyone break this thick bundle of sticks?"

    a. emphasize   **b.** accepted   **c.** inquired

4. The sons _____ the challenge, but none could do it alone.

    a. inquired   **b.** emphasize   **c.** accepted

5. However, when they were _____ and worked together, they easily broke the bundle as a team.

    a. loyal   **b.** strategy   **c.** annual

Copyright © McGraw-Hill Education. Permission is granted to reproduce for classroom use.

Vocabulary

APPLY *Antonyms* are words that mean the opposite or nearly the opposite thing. Read each word below. Write the vocabulary word that is an antonym for each word.

6. play down _____

7. unfaithful _____

8. rejected _____

Think about the meanings of *annual* and *strategy*. Use the meanings to complete each sentence below.

9. An **annual** event I like is _____

_____

_____.

10. A **strategy** for making your body stronger would be _____

_____

_____.

Copyright © McGraw-Hill Education. Permission is granted to reproduce for classroom use.

Classify and Categorize

> **FOCUS** *Classifying* and *categorizing* help you organize information. It is a way of putting people, animals, and objects into different groups. It can help you see ways things are alike and different. It can also help you remember important ideas.

PRACTICE **Think about different types of foods. Classify them into the following categories.**

Fruits

1. _____

2. _____

3. _____

Vegetables

4. _____

5. _____

6. _____

Copyright © McGraw-Hill Education. Permission is granted to reproduce for classroom use.

Classify and Categorize

APPLY In "The Bat, Birds, and Beasts" there are two teams: the Beasts and the Birds. Name two more animals that could be on each team:

7. Beasts: _____

8. Birds: _____

Think about the characters from "The Bat, Birds, and Beasts." Choose a character that belongs in each category below. Explain why you put that character in that category.

Tricky Character

9. _____

10. I put this character here because _____

_____

_____.

Big and Strong Character

11. _____

12. I put this character here because _____

_____

_____.

Access Complex Text • *Skills Practice 1*

Copyright © McGraw-Hill Education. Permission is granted to reproduce for classroom use.

Copyright © McGraw-Hill Education. Permission is granted to reproduce for classroom use.

Name _____ Date _____

Writing an Opinion Piece

Think

Audience: *Who* will read your opinion?

_____

Purpose: *What* is your reason for writing about your opinion?

_____

Prewriting

Choose reasons that support your opinion by writing your opinion, and then brainstorming reasons. Evaluate each reason, and choose the three best reasons.

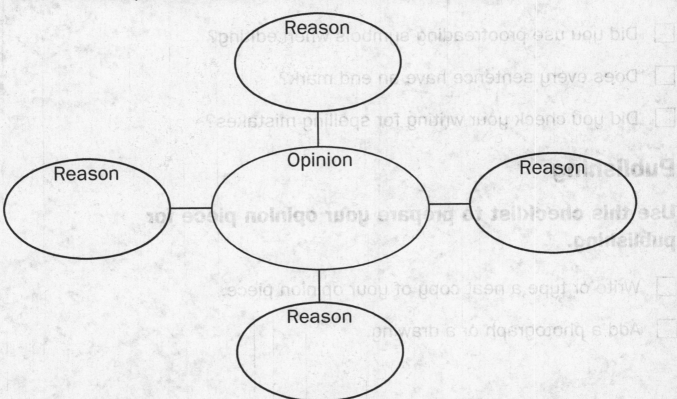

Revising

Use this checklist to revise your opinion piece.

☐ Does your writing state an opinion?

☐ Does your writing have reasons that support your opinion?

☐ Does your writing use specific vocabulary related to your topic?

☐ Does your writing present a clear point of view?

☐ Did you include an ending that sums up your opinion?

☐ Does your writing include linking words?

☐ Does your writing include detailed and descriptive language?

Editing/Proofreading

Use this checklist to correct mistakes in your opinion piece.

☐ Did you use proofreading symbols when editing?

☐ Does every sentence have an end mark?

☐ Did you check your writing for spelling mistakes?

Publishing

Use this checklist to prepare your opinion piece for publishing.

☐ Write or type a neat copy of your opinion piece.

☐ Add a photograph or a drawing.

Copyright © McGraw-Hill Education. Permission is granted to reproduce for classroom use.

Inflectional Endings -s, -es, and -ed

FOCUS
- The inflectional ending -s is added to many action verbs, but -es is added when the action verb ends in *sh, ch, s, x,* or *z*.
- The inflectional ending -ed is added to many verbs to show that the action takes place in the past. **Examples:** Emily plan**s** to study after school. Jayden watch**es** his brother play chess. Taylor's boots crunch**ed** in the snow. The flag snapp**ed** in the breeze.

PRACTICE Sort the spelling words.

Inflectional ending -s

1. _____
2. _____

Inflectional ending -es

3. _____
4. _____
5. _____

Inflectional ending -ed

6. _____
7. _____
8. _____
9. _____
10. _____

Word List		Challenge Words
1. clapped	**6.** wishes	**11.** washes
2. shops	**7.** started	**12.** refreshed
3. locked	**8.** stacks	**13.** knocks
4. patches	**9.** grabbed	**14.** guards
5. picked	**10.** pitches	**15.** called

Copyright © McGraw-Hill Education. Permission is granted to reproduce for classroom use.

APPLY Circle the correct spelling for each word.
Write the correct spelling on the line.

11. Miko (shopes, shops) for a present to give to her best friend. _____

12. Mr. Diaz (patches, patchs) holes in the tent. _____

13. My little sister (stackes, stacks) blocks and then knocks them down. _____

14. The class (wishes, wishs) it would not rain during their picnic. _____

15. Donnie (pitches, pitchs) for his baseball team. _____

Circle the correct spelling for each word. Then write the correct spelling on the line.

16. grabd   grabbed   _____

17. locked   lockt   _____

18. startid   started   _____

19. picked   pickt   _____

20. clapd   clapped   _____

Copyright © McGraw-Hill Education. Permission is granted to reproduce for classroom use.

Helping and Linking Verbs

FOCUS
- Sometimes verbs do not show action. These verbs are called linking and helping verbs.
- A **linking verb** joins, or connects, the parts of a sentence to make it complete.
  Example: There **is** a pretty shell on the beach.
- A **helping verb** helps the main verb in a sentence tell when something will happen, has happened, or is happening.
  Example: We **are** planning to look for shells.

PRACTICE Read each sentence. Write *L* if the underlined verb is a linking verb. Write *H* if the verb is a helping verb.

1. I <u>was</u> running by the ocean today. _____

2. Fish <u>are</u> swimming in the ocean. _____

3. The fish <u>was</u> by our boat. _____

4. There <u>is</u> a fish in the pond. _____

5. I <u>will</u> swim in the pond tomorrow. _____

Copyright © McGraw-Hill Education. Permission is granted to reproduce for classroom use.

APPLY Read the paragraph below. Underline the linking verbs. Circle the helping verbs.

There are more than 20,000 types of fish. I have eaten swordfish and sardines. Have you ever eaten eel? I have heard that some people eat shark. A shark is a very big fish. I have seen sharks and sea horses at the zoo. Are sea horses fish? One sea horse was a bright orange color.

Read the paragraph below. Write a linking or helping verb to complete each sentence.

There _____ six fish swimming in my aquarium. The blue fish _____ swimming faster than the orange fish. My cat _____ watching them swim. I _____ tried to teach the cat to behave. These fish _____ not for dinner, Miss Kitty! For dinner you _____ have cat food.

Copyright © McGraw-Hill Education. Permission is granted to reproduce for classroom use.

/ng/ spelled ■*ng*, /nk/ spelled ■*nk*, Inflectional Ending *-ing*

> **FOCUS** • /ng/ is a consonant sound that is spelled ■*ng*.
> • /nk/ is a consonant sound that is spelled ■*nk*.
> • The ending *-ing* lets you know something is happening now. This ending has the /ng/ sound.

PRACTICE Sort the words below. Write each word under the correct heading.

rang	hung	honk	shrunk	tank	king

/ng/	/nk/

1. _____   4. _____

2. _____   5. _____

3. _____   6. _____

Copyright © McGraw-Hill Education. Permission is granted to reproduce for classroom use.

APPLY Add *-ing* to the following words. Write each new word on the line.

7. drink _____

8. strum _____

9. nudge _____

10. jog _____

11. blend _____

12. swing _____

Write a word from the box that rhymes with each word below.

crank	chunk	banging	long	winking	link

13. stink _____

14. clanging _____

15. song _____

16. blank _____

17. dunk _____

18. thinking _____

Copyright © McGraw-Hill Education. Permission is granted to reproduce for classroom use.

Name _____ Date _____

Schwa; /əl/ spelled *el, le, al, il*

FOCUS
- The schwa sound is a vowel sound that is not stressed. The symbol for schwa is ə.
- The letters *el, le, al,* and *il* are often found at the end of words. These letter combinations make the /əl/ sound.

PRACTICE Write each word and divide it into syllables.

1. gargle _____

2. panel _____

3. metal _____

4. freckle _____

5. anvil _____

6. shrivel _____

7. shuffle _____

8. fossil _____

9. rascal _____

10. stencil _____

Copyright © McGraw-Hill Education. Permission is granted to reproduce for classroom use.

APPLY Choose a word from the box below to complete each sentence. Write the word on the line.

| puddle | model | rental | gravel | tranquil |

11. There are lots of nice _____ properties on this street.

12. The water was _____ before the storm started.

13. The teacher will _____ how to read fluently.

14. There was a _____ in our yard after the storm.

15. The parking lot is covered with _____.

Circle the word with the /əl/ sound. Then write the word on the line.

16. Ann's rings sparkle. _____

17. This novel is 350 pages long. _____

18. Dad makes a great lentil soup. _____

19. Apple tart is the best! _____

20. The tiger is my favorite animal. _____

Copyright © McGraw-Hill Education. Permission is granted to reproduce for classroom use.

Vocabulary

> ***FOCUS*** Review the vocabulary words from "A Cherokee Stickball Game."

| disappointed | furious | humbly | part | pity | roared |

***PRACTICE* Match each word with a phrase it describes.**

1. disappointed   **a.** laughing loudly

2. humbly   **b.** crying quietly over a loss

3. roared   **c.** hugging a sad friend

4. furious   **d.** not bragging

5. pity   **e.** stamping and yelling

A *base word* is a word that can stand alone. Endings are added to base words to change their meanings. Match each vocabulary word with its base word.

6. humbly   **a.** roar

7. roared   **b.** humble

8. disappointed   **c.** disappoint

Copyright © McGraw-Hill Education. Permission is granted to reproduce for classroom use.

Vocabulary

APPLY Use the vocabulary words to complete
the story below.

Why Rabbit Has a Short Tail
A Cherokee Folktale

Long ago Rabbit had a long tail. Rabbit was always
bragging about it. This made Fox angry. Fox became so
9. _____ that he decided to trick Rabbit.

Fox went to the middle of a frozen lake. He cut a
hole in the ice. He tied fish to his tail and put
10. _____ of his tail through the hole. When
Rabbit came by, Fox said he was fishing. He lied
and said he had caught many fish this way.

Rabbit wanted to try. However, Rabbit kept his tail in
the cold water too long. It froze! Fox pretended to take
11. _____ on Rabbit, and he pulled Rabbit.
He pulled so hard that Rabbit's long tail broke off.
Then Fox **12.** _____ with laughter.

Rabbit was no longer proud. He hopped
13. _____ off. Ever since, poor Rabbit has
been **14.** _____ in his short, stubby tail.

Copyright © McGraw-Hill Education. Permission is granted to reproduce for classroom use.

Sequence

> ## FOCUS
> *Sequence* is the order in which events happen in a story. Writers often use time and order words to help readers understand sequence.
>
> - **Time words:** today, summer, night, hour, minute
> - **Order words:** first, next, finally

PRACTICE Read the following sentences. Draw a line under each *time* and *order* word. Then put numbers in front of the sentences to show the order in which they belong.

1. _____ Yesterday, the children decided to go ice-skating.

2. _____ Finally, they went home.

3. _____ First they put on their warm clothes.

4. _____ Next they walked to the ice-skating rink.

5. _____ They skated for an hour.

6. _____ After they were home, they were so tired that they went straight to bed.

Copyright © McGraw-Hill Education. Permission is granted to reproduce for classroom use.

Sequence

APPLY Think about the plot of "A Cherokee Stickball Game." Use what you know from the text to answer the sequence questions below.

7. What was the first thing the story tells us about stickball?

_____

Recount, or retell, the order of events from the game. Use the order words *first*, *next*, and *finally*.

8. _____

9. _____

10. _____

11. What was the last thing Little Mouse/Flying Bat did in the story?

_____

Think about your answer for #7. Think about what you know about Flying Bat. Use those things to make an inference, or educated guess, about what Flying Bat did after the end of the story.

12. _____

Access Complex Text • *Skills Practice 1*

Copyright © McGraw-Hill Education. Permission is granted to reproduce for classroom use.

Writing an Opinion Piece

Think

Audience: *Who* will read your opinion?

_____

_____

Purpose: *What* is your reason for writing about
your opinion?

_____

_____

Prewriting

Plan your opinion piece by choosing your topic and
forming three opinions about your topic. Then write
the opinions below.

Copyright © McGraw-Hill Education. Permission is granted to reproduce for classroom use.

Revising

Use this checklist to revise your opinion piece.

☐ Does your writing state an opinion?

☐ Does your writing have reasons that support your opinion?

☐ Does your writing include specific vocabulary related to your topic?

☐ Did you include words that make your point of view clear?

☐ Did you include an ending that sums up your opinion?

☐ Did you include words and phrases to show that it is an opinion piece?

☐ Does your writing include linking words?

Editing/Proofreading

Use this checklist to correct mistakes in your opinion piece.

☐ Did you use proofreading symbols when editing?

☐ Did you check your writing for spelling mistakes?

Publishing

Use this checklist to prepare your opinion piece for publishing.

☐ Write or type a neat copy of your opinion piece.

☐ Add a photograph or a drawing.

☐ Read your opinion piece to the class or to a small group of classmates.

Copyright © McGraw-Hill Education. Permission is granted to reproduce for classroom use.

/ng/ spelled ∎ng; /nk/ spelled ∎nk; inflectional ending -ing; /əl/ spelled el, le, al, and il

FOCUS
- One way to spell /ng/ is ∎ng.
- One way to spell /nk/ is ∎nk.
- When a sentence uses a helping verb, the inflectional ending -ing is often added to the main verb.
- /əl/ can be spelled el, le, al, and il.

PRACTICE Sort the spelling words under the correct heading.

/ng/ spelled ∎ng

1. _____

/əl/ spelled le

2. _____

3. _____

/əl/ spelled el

4. _____

/nk/ spelled ∎nk

5. _____

6. _____

7. _____

8. _____

Inflectional ending -ing

9. _____

10. _____

Word List		Challenge Words
1. think	**6.** sink	**11.** barrel
2. middle	**7.** gravel	**12.** civil
3. rushing	**8.** shrank	**13.** going
4. strong	**9.** grinning	**14.** normal
5. pickle	**10.** blank	**15.** flying

Copyright © McGraw-Hill Education. Permission is granted to reproduce for classroom use.

APPLY Fill in the blank with a spelling word from the box.

gravel	strong	think	blank	middle

11. Devon will _____ of a way to teach his dog to fetch.

12. Are you _____ enough to lift that brick?

13. A truck dumped a pile of _____ in front of the building.

14. The _____ of the casserole was still cold, so we baked it another ten minutes.

15. Nola drew a happy face in the _____ space of her paper.

Circle the correct spelling for each word. Write the correctly spelled word on the line.

16. rushing   rushink   _____

17. sinc   sink   _____

18. pickil   pickle   _____

19. shrangk   shrank   _____

20. grinning   grinin   _____

Copyright © McGraw-Hill Education. Permission is granted to reproduce for classroom use.

Subject and Predicate

FOCUS
- A **sentence** is a group of words that expresses a complete thought. A sentence has two parts: a naming part and a telling part.
- The **subject** of a sentence includes all the words in the naming part.
  Example: The game of soccer
- The **predicate** includes all the words in the telling part.
  Example: is played around the world.

PRACTICE For each sentence, underline the *subject* once and the *predicate* twice.

1. Soccer began in England in the 1800s.

2. Two teams of eleven players each compete in soccer.

3. The players try to put a ball into the other team's goal.

4. The goals are two nets at opposite ends of a rectangular field.

5. Each goal is worth one point to the team that scored.

Copyright © McGraw-Hill Education. Permission is granted to reproduce for classroom use.

APPLY Read each sentence. Write *S* on the line if
the underlined part is a subject, and write *P* if it
is a predicate.

6. <u>The game of rugby</u> uses an oval-shaped ball.

_____

7. The players on a rugby team <u>carry, kick, or pass</u>

<u>the ball.</u> _____

8. Fifteen players <u>make up a team</u>. _____

9. <u>The object of the game</u> is to score goals.

_____

10. The team with the ball <u>is the offensive team</u>.

_____

11. <u>The game of football</u> was developed from the English

game of rugby. _____

12. <u>The team trying to stop the offensive team</u> is the

defensive team. _____

**Write three sentences. Underline the *subject* once and
the *predicate* twice.**

13. _____

14. _____

15. _____

Copyright © McGraw-Hill Education. Permission is granted to reproduce for classroom use.

/er/ spelled *er, ir, ur, ear*

> **FOCUS**
> • When *r* follows the letters *e, i, u,* or *a*, it usually makes the /er/ sound.
> • The /er/ sound can also be spelled *ear*.

PRACTICE Sort the words under the correct heading.

slurp	heard	shirt	verb	girl	buzzer	turnip	earn

/er/ spelled *er*

1. _____

2. _____

/er/ spelled *ir*

3. _____

4. _____

/er/ spelled *ur*

5. _____

6. _____

/er/ spelled *ear*

7. _____

8. _____

Copyright © McGraw-Hill Education. Permission is granted to reproduce for classroom use.

APPLY Write *er*, *ir*, *ur*, or *ear* to complete each word.

9. p_____ple

10. wh_____l

11. p_____mit

12. k_____nel

13. s_____ch

14. b_____st

Circle the word or words with /er/. Write each word on the line.

15. Jess is turning seven!

_____

16. Cam lost his sister's ring.

_____

17. Stir the pot to mix in the milk.

_____

18. Bill can earn eight dollars cutting grass.

_____

Copyright © McGraw-Hill Education. Permission is granted to reproduce for classroom use.

/or/ spelled *or, ore*

> **FOCUS** /or/ is a special vowel sound that can be spelled *or* and *ore*.

PRACTICE Replace the underlined letter or letters to make a word with the *ore* spelling.

1. bor<u>n</u> + e = _____

2. stor<u>m</u> + e = _____

3. por<u>t</u> + e = _____

4. tor<u>ch</u> + e = _____

5. cor<u>k</u> + e = _____

Replace the letter *e* with the new letter or letters to make a word with the *or* spelling.

6. bor<u>e</u> + der = _____

7. stor<u>e</u> + y = _____

8. por<u>e</u> + tal = _____

9. tor<u>e</u> + n = _____

10. cor<u>e</u> + n = _____

Copyright © McGraw-Hill Education. Permission is granted to reproduce for classroom use.

APPLY Choose a word from the box below to complete each sentence. Write the word on the line.

fork	horse	wore	adore	short

11. Dad _____ a cap to the game.

12. Pack a _____ in the picnic basket.

13. It is just a _____ walk to the store.

14. We _____ our little kitten.

15. The _____ trotted into the barn.

Draw a line matching a word on the left to a rhyming word on the right.

16. cord   **a.** chore

17. form   **b.** storm

18. forecast   **c.** escort

19. support   **d.** bored

20. shore   **e.** contrast

Vocabulary

> **FOCUS** Review the vocabulary words from "The Final Game."

broke	eagerness	opponent	sneered
checked	grandstand	piercing	tense
commotion	managed		

PRACTICE Match each vocabulary word with its definition.

1. piercing   **a.** said something that showed hatred

2. tense   **b.** noisy confusion

3. broke   **c.** making a sharp sound

4. checked   **d.** a person who is against another

5. grandstand   **e.** causing suspense

6. opponent   **f.** the main place where people sit when watching a sports event

7. commotion   **g.** caused to end

8. sneered   **h.** stopped another player from going forward

Copyright © McGraw-Hill Education. Permission is granted to reproduce for classroom use.

Vocabulary

APPLY A *base word* is a word that can stand alone. Endings are added to base words to change their meanings. Use this information to complete the following activities.

9. What is the base word of *checked*?

_____

10. List another word with the same base.

_____

11. What is the base word of *managed*?

_____

12. List another word with the same base.

_____

13. What is the base word of *piercing*?

_____

14. List another word with the same base.

_____

15. What is the base word of *eagerness*?

_____

16. List another word with the same base.

_____

Copyright © McGraw-Hill Education. Permission is granted to reproduce for classroom use.

Making Inferences

> ***FOCUS*** When you *make inferences,* you use information provided in a text, along with what you already know, to understand details the author did not put in the story.

PRACTICE Read each group of sentences. Circle the correct *inference*.

1. Zoe shivered. She went and found a sweater. After she put the sweater on, she decided to put a jacket on, too.

Inference:

   a. Zoe was cold.   **b.** Zoe felt sad.

2. The teddy bear had lost most of its stuffing. One eye was missing. Its ear was torn.

Inference:

   a. The teddy bear was old.   **b.** The teddy bear was lost.

3. Jacob bounced up and down. He could not stop smiling. Every few minutes he ran to look out the window.

Inference:

   a. Jacob is excited about going to bed.   **b.** Jacob is excited about someone coming to visit.

Copyright © McGraw-Hill Education. Permission is granted to reproduce for classroom use.

Making Inferences

APPLY Read each quote from "The Final Game." Use what you already know to answer each question that follows and make an inference.

> "I jumped out of bed and ran to the window. Over the rooftops a plume of white smoke billowed in the distance. My heart leapt. I had forgotten! My brother was on that train."

4. What inference can you make about how Moccasin Danny feels toward his brother?

_____

5. What information from the text helped you?

_____

6. What did you already know that helped you?

_____

> "...the Bombers scored on me. I looked at our bench. Bob and Coach Matteau just shook their heads."

7. What inference can you make about Bob and Coach Matteau's feelings?

_____

8. What information did you use to make this inference?

_____

Access Complex Text • *Skills Practice 1*

Copyright © McGraw-Hill Education. Permission is granted to reproduce for classroom use.

Writing an Opinion Piece

Think

Audience: *Who* will read your opinion?

_____

Purpose: *What* is your reason for writing about your opinion?

_____

Prewriting

Use the space below to list positive and negative words that might describe the topic of your opinion piece. Be sure to choose words from the list that support your point of view about the topic.

Topic: _____

Positive words   **Negative words**

Copyright © McGraw-Hill Education. Permission is granted to reproduce for classroom use.

Proofreading Symbols

¶   Indent the paragraph.

^   Add something.

℘   Take out something.

/   Make a small letter.

≡   Make a capital letter.

sp   Check spelling.

⊙   Add a period.

Copyright © McGraw-Hill Education. Permission is granted to reproduce for classroom use.

/er/ spelled *er, ir, ur;* /or/ spelled *or, ore*

> **FOCUS** • The /er/ sound can be spelled *er, ir,* and *ur.*
> • The /or/ sound can be spelled *or* and *ore.*

PRACTICE Sort the spelling words under the correct heading.

/er/ spelled *er*

1. _____

2. _____

/or/ spelled *or*

6. _____

7. _____

/er/ spelled *ir*

3. _____

4. _____

/or/ spelled *ore*

8. _____

9. _____

10. _____

/er/ spelled *ur*

5. _____

Word List		**Challenge Words**
1. bird	**6.** stork	**11.** ignored
2. chores	**7.** purple	**12.** forest
3. short	**8.** whirling	**13.** mother
4. antlers	**9.** perched	**14.** served
5. snored	**10.** explore	**15.** flowers

Copyright © McGraw-Hill Education. Permission is granted to reproduce for classroom use.

APPLY Replace the underlined letter or letters to create a spelling word with the same /er/ or /or/ spelling. Write the word on the line.

11. <u>f</u>ort + sh = _____

12. <u>th</u>ird + b = _____

13. <u>b</u>ored + sn = _____

14. <u>tw</u>irling + wh = _____

15. <u>sh</u>ores + ch = _____

Circle the correct spelling for each spelling word. Write the correct spelling on the line.

16. percht   perched   _____

17. perpel   purple   _____

18. explore   exsplor   _____

19. storek   stork   _____

20. antlers   antlurs   _____

Spelling • *Skills Practice 1*

Capitalization: First Word of a Sentence

> **FOCUS**
> - Capital letters are used in many places. One place capital letters are used is at the beginnings of sentences.
> - A sentence always begins with a capital letter.
>   **Examples: C**amping is fun. **H**ave you ever slept outside?

PRACTICE Triple-underline the beginning letter of each sentence.

did you know that the teddy bear is over one hundred years old? this popular toy has been around longer than the electric light, telephone, and motor car. in 1902, President Theodore Roosevelt was on a hunting trip and had the chance to shoot a captured bear. he refused, saying "Spare the bear!" a cartoon was drawn of this event and put in the newspaper. two shopkeepers, Morris and Rose Michtom, made a soft bear, which they called Teddy's Bear. the teddy bear was an overnight success and is still very popular today.

Copyright © McGraw-Hill Education. Permission is granted to reproduce for classroom use.

APPLY Write a paragraph about your favorite toy.
After writing, go back and circle the first letter of
each sentence. Make sure it is a capital letter.

_____

_____

_____

_____

_____

_____

_____

Triple-underline the letters that should be capital letters.

Dear Lucas,

    i had a great time visiting you. it was fun to play
video games and ride our bikes. your sister, Amelia,
was fun too. next time maybe we can go in your tree
fort. please tell your mom thank you for letting me
come to visit.

                          Sincerely,

                          Noah

Copyright © McGraw-Hill Education. Permission is granted to reproduce for classroom use.

Name _____ Date _____

Fluency Checklist

As you read the passage on the next page, be sure to keep the following things in mind to help you read with the appropriate rate, accuracy, and expression.

As you read, make sure you

☐ pause longer at a period or other ending punctuation.

☐ raise your voice at a question mark.

☐ use expression when you come to an exclamation point.

☐ pause at commas but not as long as you would at a period.

☐ think of the character and how he or she might say his or her words whenever you come to quotation marks.

☐ remember not to read so fast that someone listening cannot hear the individual words or make sense of what is being read.

☐ stop and reread something that does not make sense.

Skills Practice 1 • Fluency

UNIT 1 • Lesson 6 **71**

A Trip

Dad, Mom, and the kids went on a trip. They packed the van before they left. Dad grabbed bags until the van could fit no more.

Mom packed lunches, water, and snacks. She did not want to stop on the trip. The kids packed things to help them have fun for the long ride.

Traveling turned out to be fun! They went up and down hills. They went in and out of tunnels. Mom asked the kids if they wanted to sing. They said no thanks.

When the van stopped, the kids looked to see where they were. They saw a big forest. What would happen next? Dad jumped out of the van and started to unpack. The first things he grabbed were the tents. They would camp on this trip!

After the tents were finished, they set up their cots. The kids filled their packs. They wanted to explore the forest. Mom and Dad went with them.

They discovered lots of things in the forest. The best thing was seeing two elks by the water. It was a good first day of camping, and they had four more days to go.

Copyright © McGraw-Hill Education. Permission is granted to reproduce for classroom use.

Name _____ **Date** _____

Vocabulary

> **FOCUS** Review the vocabulary words from "Ellie's Long Walk."

adopt	journey	slope
entire	panic	startled
face	raged	surface
inch	slick	turned

PRACTICE Circle the word in parentheses that best fits each sentence.

1. The family packed their car to get ready for their (surface/**journey**).

2. Once all the bags were inside, the (panic/**entire**) backseat was full.

3. The mother was in a (**panic**/startled) as she cried out, "Where will the children sit?"

4. "Relax," the father said. "Let's (turned/**face**) the problem and find a solution."

5. It was the children, however, who found the missing car top carrier that attached to the (adopt/**surface**) of the roof.

Vocabulary

APPLY A *simile* compares two unlike things. It includes the words *like* or *as*. Use a vocabulary word to complete each simile below.

6. _____ as ice

7. _____ like an angry bull

Use what you know about each vocabulary word to answer the following questions.

8. If you *adopt* a good attitude, what does that mean? _____

9. If you roll a ball down a *slope,* will the ball go faster or slower? _____

10. If you clean every *inch* of your room, do you clean it well or sloppily? _____

11. If you are *startled,* are you calm or surprised? _____

12. If weather *turned* hot, did the weather stay the same or change? _____

Copyright © McGraw-Hill Education. Permission is granted to reproduce for classroom use.

Main Idea and Details

<table>
<tr>
<td>

FOCUS

</td>
<td>

- The *main idea* tells what a paragraph is about. It is the most important idea presented by the author.

- *Details* provide more specific information about the *main idea*.

</td>
</tr>
</table>

PRACTICE Read each paragraph. They are each missing the main idea sentence. Circle the *main idea* that goes with each group of *details*.

1. Hikers need to bring plenty of food. They also need to bring tools to clean drinking water. Everything will be in their packs, so they do not want things that are too heavy.

   Main Idea:

   a. Hikers need to prepare thoroughly when going on a long hike.

   b. Hikers should never hike alone.

2. Dogs are loyal to their owners. They can be trained to follow commands. They are very smart.

   Main Idea:

   a. Dogs make good pets.

   b. Dogs and cats are both good kinds of pets.

Copyright © McGraw-Hill Education. Permission is granted to reproduce for classroom use.

Main Idea and Details

APPLY Read each main idea below. For each main idea, write two sentences that give details from "Ellie's Long Walk" that support the main idea.

Pam and Ellie liked each other right away.

Details that support this idea:

3. _____

_____

4. _____

_____

Pam took her time training Ellie before their hike.

Details that support this idea:

5. _____

_____

6. _____

_____

Ellie and Pam were scared during the big storm in October.

Details that support this idea:

7. _____

8. _____

Copyright © McGraw-Hill Education. Permission is granted to reproduce for classroom use.

/ā/ spelled *a* and *a_e*

> **FOCUS** The /ā/ sound can be spelled with *a* and *a_e*.

PRACTICE Read the following words. Underline the *a* or *a_e* spelling pattern used in each word.

1. basic
2. rake
3. fade
4. staple

5. cane
6. favor
7. able
8. basis

Replace the underlined letters with the given letter or letters to create a rhyming word. The new word will have the same spelling for /ā/. Write the new word on the line.

9. <u>f</u>able + t = _____

10. <u>w</u>ave + g = _____

11. <u>l</u>ake + f = _____

12. <u>m</u>ade + f = _____

13. <u>c</u>able + st = _____

14. <u>v</u>ase + c = _____

Copyright © McGraw-Hill Education. Permission is granted to reproduce for classroom use.

APPLY Choose a word from the box below to complete each sentence. Write the word on the line.

bacon	taste	makes	trade	table	apron

15. My favorite breakfast is eggs and _____.

16. I will _____ you my apple for your banana.

17. Will you please set the _____ for dinner?

18. Aunt Kate _____ the best salads.

19. Dad wears an _____ when he is cooking.

20. Kathy can't wait to _____ the pasta.

Circle the correct spelling of each word.

21. baceon   bacon

22. fake   fak

23. date   daet

24. laybal   label

25. naem   name

26. rake   raek

Copyright © McGraw-Hill Education. Permission is granted to reproduce for classroom use.

/ī/ spelled *i* and *i_e*

FOCUS The /ī/ sound can be spelled with *i* and *i_e*.

PRACTICE Read the following words out loud.
Underline the *i* or *i_e* spelling pattern used in
each word.

1. idol

5. side

2. ride

6. pilot

3. item

7. hike

4. pipe

8. iris

**Write two sentences using any of the words spelled
with *i* and *i_e* from above.**

9. _____

_____

10. _____

_____

Copyright © McGraw-Hill Education. Permission is granted to reproduce for classroom use.

APPLY Choose a word from the box below to complete each sentence. Write the word on the line.

silent	time	dime	virus	kite	child

11. What _____ do you wake up?

12. A _____ is worth ten cents.

13. A _____ can make you feel sick.

14. Miles let his _____ rise in the wind.

15. The _____ sat on her mom's lap.

16. We must stay _____ when others are speaking.

Circle the correct spelling of each word.

17. blined   blind

18. fier   fire

19. wise   wis

20. ireon   iron

21. side   sid

22. rise   ries

Copyright © McGraw-Hill Education. Permission is granted to reproduce for classroom use.

Vocabulary

| FOCUS | Review the vocabulary words from "Mattland." |

cleared	jagged	peaks	prickly	tufts
culverts	pasture	plucking	smoothed	wind

PRACTICE Match each vocabulary word with its example.

1. plucking

a. rubbed away a rough spot

2. smoothed

b. tops of mountains

3. pasture

c. picking flowers

4. culverts

d. thorns on a cactus

5. wind

e. a meadow

6. jagged

f. wrapping string around

7. peaks

g. rough, broken glass

8. prickly

h. water draining under a road

Copyright © McGraw-Hill Education. Permission is granted to reproduce for classroom use.

Vocabulary

APPLY Read the following paragraph. Decide whether the underlined words make sense as they are used. If an underlined word does not make sense, cross it out and replace it with the correct vocabulary word. If an underlined word is used correctly, write *correct*.

A topographic map is a special kind of map. It has lines on it that show the <u>tufts</u> **9.** _____ and valleys on Earth's surface. Many <u>jagged</u> **10.** _____ lines close together might show a steep mountain. If there are few lines, it might show a flat <u>pasture</u> **11.** _____ or other piece of <u>cleared</u> **12.** _____ land.

Use your knowledge of the vocabulary words to answer each question.

13. Would *tuft*s of yarn be big or small? _____

14. If a boy is *plucking* grass, is he planting it or pulling it out?

_____

15. If you *smoothed* a blanket, did you make it flat or bumpy?

_____

Copyright © McGraw-Hill Education. Permission is granted to reproduce for classroom use.

Making Inferences

> **FOCUS** When you *make inferences*, you use information provided in a text, along with what you already know, to understand details the author did not put in the story.

PRACTICE Read each description. Circle the *inference* that makes sense.

1. In the distance, thunder rumbled. The thunder grew louder.

   Inference: a. A storm is over.   **b.** A storm is coming.

2. Carmen looked away from her friend. She felt her face get hot. She did not say anything.

   Inference: a. Carmen is embarrassed.   **b.** Carmen is sleepy.

3. The sun peeked over the hill. The light grew ever brighter.

   Inference: a. The sun is rising.   **b.** The sun is setting.

4. Hakeem smiled at his little brother. He handed him some toys. "Let's play," Hakeem said.

   Inference: a. Hakeem is patient.   **b.** Hakeem is annoyed.

Copyright © McGraw-Hill Education. Permission is granted to reproduce for classroom use.

Making Inferences

APPLY Think about the main character in "Mattland." Then read the following paragraph. Make two inferences telling about ways these characters are the same. Explain your reasons, using details from each text.

Hilary dragged her feet on the ground. She did not look up when she passed other kids on their way to school. Why did she have to start a new school now, in the middle of the year? She wanted to throw her backpack on the ground and run away.

5. Inference: _____

6. Why I made this inference: _____

7. Inference: _____

8. Why I made this inference: _____

Copyright © McGraw-Hill Education. Permission is granted to reproduce for classroom use.

Copyright © McGraw-Hill Education. Permission is granted to reproduce for classroom use.

Name _____ Date _____

Writing to Inform

Think

Audience: *Who* will read your writing?

_____

Purpose: *What* is your reason for writing about your topic?

_____

Practice

Varying the types of sentences you use in your writing will make it more interesting to read. Write four different types of sentences about your topic.

Topic: _____

1. **Declarative:** _____

_____

2. **Interrogative:** _____

_____

3. **Imperative:** _____

_____

4. **Exclamatory:** _____

_____

Revising

Use this checklist to revise your writing.

☐ Does your writing have a topic sentence?

☐ Does your writing have facts that describe your topic?

☐ Did you vary the kinds of sentences you wrote?

☐ Did you include an ending that sums up your topic?

Editing/Proofreading

Use this checklist to correct mistakes in your writing.

☐ Did you use proofreading symbols when editing?

☐ Did you use the correct end marks for different sentence types?

☐ Did you check your writing for spelling mistakes?

Publishing

Use this checklist to publish your writing.

☐ Write or type a neat copy of your writing.

☐ Add a photograph or a drawing.

Copyright © McGraw-Hill Education. Permission is granted to reproduce for classroom use.

/ā/ spelled *a* and *a_e*;/ī/ spelled *i* and *i_e*

FOCUS
- Long vowels sound like their names.
- Two ways /ā/ can be spelled are *a* and *a_e*.
- Two ways /ī/ can be spelled are *i* and *i_e*.

PRACTICE Sort the spelling words.

/ā/ spelled *a*

1. _____

2. _____

/ā/ spelled *a_e*

3. _____

4. _____

5. _____

/ī/ spelled *i*

6. _____

7. _____

8. _____

/ī/ spelled *i_e*

9. _____

10. _____

Word List		**Challenge Words**
1. mild	**6.** time	**11.** apron
2. pale	**7.** sale	**12.** final
3. pilot	**8.** ride	**13.** became
4. paper	**9.** able	**14.** radar
5. bake	**10.** kind	**15.** while

Copyright © McGraw-Hill Education. Permission is granted to reproduce for classroom use.

APPLY

Write the spelling word that rhymes with each set of words below. The new word should have the same spelling pattern.

11. stale   male   _____

12. rake   make   _____

13. side   hide   _____

14. cable   table   _____

15. wild   child   _____

Circle the correct spelling for each spelling word. Write the correct spelling on the line.

16. pilot   pylot   _____

17. paeper   paper   _____

18. kinde   kind   _____

19. sael   sale   _____

20. time   tiem   _____

Spelling • *Skills Practice 1*

Complete and Incomplete Sentences

> **FOCUS**
> - A **complete sentence** has a subject and a predicate.
> - In an **incomplete sentence,** or **fragment,** the subject or predicate is missing.
> - To *correct* an incomplete sentence, add the missing subject or predicate to the sentence.
>
> **Example:**
> Fragment: More than one billion vehicles.
> Correct: More than one billion vehicles have crossed the bridge.

PRACTICE Circle the word group that correctly completes each sentence.

1. The first bridges were tree trunks.
some footbridges.

2. Pontoon boats the surface.
float on the water.

3. Arches are very strong.
curved supports.

4. The cars go quickly down the road.
quick and fast.

5. The rushing river by the park.
took the boat downstream.

Copyright © McGraw-Hill Education. Permission is granted to reproduce for classroom use.

APPLY Read the following. Write *C* for a complete sentence and *I* for an incomplete sentence.

6. Orange trees plenty of water. _____

7. Potatoes grow in cool climates. _____

8. My family garden. _____

9. Like to grow green peppers. _____

10. Flower in our yard. _____

Correctly rewrite each of the incomplete sentences from above.

11. _____

_____

12. _____

_____

13. _____

_____

14. _____

_____

Copyright © McGraw-Hill Education. Permission is granted to reproduce for classroom use.

/ō/ spelled *o* and *o_e*

> **FOCUS** The /ō/ sound can be spelled with *o* and *o_e*.

PRACTICE Replace the beginning letter of each word with one of the following letters to make a new rhyming word. Write the new word on the line. Use each letter one time.

j	d	r	w	m	s

1. no _____

2. nose _____

3. home _____

4. rove _____

5. host _____

6. poke _____

Use the pairs of words above to complete the following sentences. Write the words on the lines.

7. Use your _____ to smell the _____.

8. _____ parties will have a _____.

9. My mom said _____, _____ I cannot go to the park.

10. It's no _____ to get a _____ in the eye.

Copyright © McGraw-Hill Education. Permission is granted to reproduce for classroom use.

APPLY Read the word in the box. Then read the sentence. Change the word in the box to make a new rhyming word that will complete the sentence. Write the word on the line.

11. | cone | My dog loves to chew on his _____.

12. | toll | Mona put butter on the warm _____.

13. | fold | The man on the corner _____ hot dogs.

14. | role | We dug a _____ in the backyard.

15. | bolt | Suddenly, the car stopped with a _____.

16. | nose | I watered the lawn with a _____.

Circle the correct spelling of each word.

17. sold   soled

18. oveal   oval

19. ohw   owe

20. pose   pos

21. toen   tone

22. old   oled

Copyright © McGraw-Hill Education. Permission is granted to reproduce for classroom use.

/ū/ spelled *u* and *u_e*

FOCUS The /ū/ sound can be spelled with *u* and *u_e*.

PRACTICE Read each sentence. Circle the word that correctly completes the sentence.

1. I don't like the _____ at the gas station.

                 fyumz   fumes

2. The _____ baby smiled at us.

          cute   cut

3. Utah is one of the fifty _____ States of America.

                    Uneited   United

4. I _____ to give up.

   refuse   refus

Circle the correct spelling of each word.

5. menu   menue

6. myusic   music

7. cueb   cube

8. fuse   fues

Copyright © McGraw-Hill Education. Permission is granted to reproduce for classroom use.

APPLY Use each word in the box in a sentence. Write the sentence on the lines.

cute	humid	pupil	mule	mute	bugle

9. _____

_____

10. _____

_____

11. _____

_____

12. _____

_____

13. _____

_____

14. _____

_____

Copyright © McGraw-Hill Education. Permission is granted to reproduce for classroom use.

Phonics • *Skills Practice 1*

Vocabulary

> **FOCUS** Review the vocabulary words from "A River of Ice."

crevasse	glacier	over	rub	time
fjords	happens	press	scratch	valley

PRACTICE Use what you know about the vocabulary words to answer each question.

1. Does land go down or up into a *valley*? _____

2. Is a *crevasse* a hill or a deep hole? _____

3. If you *press* on thin ice, will it break? _____

4. Is a *glacier* mostly made of rock or ice? _____

5. Could an animal's claw *scratch* mud? _____

6. If you are outside when a rainstorm *happens*, will you get wet? _____

Copyright © McGraw-Hill Education. Permission is granted to reproduce for classroom use.

Vocabulary

APPLY Answer the following questions about
"A River of Ice."

7. Explain what a *crevasse* is. Use the word *happens* in your
   explanation. _____

   _____

8. Explain how *fjords* are made. Use the words *scratch* and *over*
   in your explanation. _____

   _____

**Hyperbole is a way of using words to exaggerate, or
overstate, something. Read each sentence below.
Then explain what the speaker really meant to say.**

9. I am so broke that I don't have two pennies to rub
   together. _____

   _____

10. That joke is so old, that last time I heard it I was riding
    a dinosaur. _____

    _____

Copyright © McGraw-Hill Education. Permission is granted to reproduce for classroom use.

Main Idea and Details

FOCUS
- The *main idea* tells what a paragraph or section is about. It is the most important idea presented by the author.
- *Details* provide more specific information about the *main idea*.

PRACTICE Read each main idea below. Circle the *detail* that goes with each main idea.

1. Frostbite can be prevented.

   a. Frost can make pretty patterns on glass.

   b. People should wear several layers of warm clothing in cold weather.

2. Long ago, Antarctica was a warm place.

   a. Ancient shells show that Antarctica once had weather like California.

   b. Antarctica is home to several types of penguins.

Write two details for the main idea: *Summer is fun*.

3. _____

4. _____

Copyright © McGraw-Hill Education. Permission is granted to reproduce for classroom use.

Main Idea and Details

APPLY Look through "A River of Ice." Find a main idea sentence and write it on the line below.

5. Main Idea: _____

Now write three details that go with this main idea.

Details

6. _____

7. _____

8. _____

Copyright © McGraw-Hill Education. Permission is granted to reproduce for classroom use.

Access Complex Text • *Skills Practice 1*

Writing to Inform

Think

Audience: *Who* will read your writing?

_____

_____

Purpose: *What* is your reason for writing about your topic?

_____

_____

Practice

Staying on topic is important. Read the group of sentences below each topic. Cross out the sentence that does not stay on topic.

1. **Topic:** The California Gold Rush

   Gold was discovered at Sutter's Mill in 1848.
   Approximately 300,000 people raced to California in search for gold.
   Today, an ounce of silver is worth about sixteen dollars.
   Gold miners lived a hard life, often living for weeks in primitive camps.

2. **Topic:** Bees

   Bees are found on every continent except Antarctica.
   Some wasps build their nests out of mud, while others use chewed-up wood.
   Many plants are pollinated by bees.
   Bumblebees make honey, but they do not make enough for humans to use.

Copyright © McGraw-Hill Education. Permission is granted to reproduce for classroom use.

Revising

Use this checklist to revise your writing.

- [ ] Does your writing have a topic sentence?

- [ ] Does your writing have facts that describe your topic?

- [ ] Did you use descriptive words to make the topic interesting?

- [ ] Did you include an ending that sums up your topic?

Editing/Proofreading

Use this checklist to correct mistakes in your writing.

- [ ] Did you use proofreading symbols when editing?

- [ ] Did you use complete sentences?

- [ ] Did you include an end mark for each sentence?

- [ ] Did you check your writing for spelling mistakes?

Publishing

Use this checklist to publish your writing.

- [ ] Write or type a neat copy of your writing.

- [ ] Add a photograph or a drawing.

Copyright © McGraw-Hill Education. Permission is granted to reproduce for classroom use.

/ō/ spelled o and o_e; /ū/ spelled u and u_e

> **FOCUS** • Long vowels sound like their names.
> • Two ways /ō/ can be spelled are o and o_e.
> • Two ways /ū/ can be spelled are u and u_e.

PRACTICE Sort the spelling words.

/ō/ spelled o

1. _____

2. _____

/ō/ spelled o_e

3. _____

4. _____

5. _____

/ū/ spelled u

6. _____

7. _____

/ū/ spelled u_e

8. _____

9. _____

10. _____

Word List		**Challenge Words**
1. menu	**6.** unit	**11.** stone
2. nose	**7.** vote	**12.** bugle
3. most	**8.** fuse	**13.** total
4. cube	**9.** over	**14.** hugest
5. joke	**10.** mule	**15.** suppose

Copyright © McGraw-Hill Education. Permission is granted to reproduce for classroom use.

APPLY

Replace the underlined letter or letters to create a spelling word. The new word will have the same spelling pattern for /ō/.

11. <u>n</u>ote + v = _____

12. <u>h</u>ost + m = _____

13. <u>c</u>hose + n = _____

14. <u>b</u>roke + j = _____

Circle the correct spelling for each spelling word. Write the correct spelling on the line.

15. oever   over   _____

16. menu   menyou   _____

17. mule   myool   _____

18. kyube   cube   _____

19. phuse   fuse   _____

20. unit   younet   _____

Copyright © McGraw-Hill Education. Permission is granted to reproduce for classroom use.

Kinds of Sentences and End Marks

> **FOCUS**
> - There are different kinds of sentences.
> - A **declarative sentence** makes a statement. It ends with a period (.).
> - An **interrogative sentence** asks a question. It ends with a question mark (?).
> - An **imperative sentence** gives a direction or a command. It ends with a period (.).
> - An **exclamatory sentence** shows strong feeling. It ends with an exclamation point (!).

PRACTICE Read each sentence below. Write the type of sentence on the line.

1. Pick up that rock. _____

2. Did you find any rocks today? _____

3. Rocks can be all different sizes. _____

4. I love collecting rocks! _____

5. Have you ever seen a red rock? _____

6. I have ten rocks in my collection. _____

7. Stop! _____

8. I had an awesome time! _____

Copyright © McGraw-Hill Education. Permission is granted to reproduce for classroom use.

APPLY Write an example of each type of sentence
listed below. Make sure to use the correct end mark
for each type of sentence.

9. (exclamatory) _____

_____

10. (interrogative) _____

_____

11. (declarative) _____

_____

12. (imperative) _____

_____

13. (exclamatory) _____

_____

14. (interrogative) _____

_____

15. (declarative) _____

_____

16. (imperative) _____

_____

Grammar • *Skills Practice 1*

Copyright © McGraw-Hill Education. Permission is granted to reproduce for classroom use.

Long Vowels, Inflectional Endings
-er and -est

FOCUS
- The /ā/ sound can be spelled with *a* and *a_e*.
- The /ī/ sound can be spelled with *i* and *i_e*.
- The /ō/ sound can be spelled with *o* and *o_e*.
- The /ū/ sound can be spelled with *u* and *u_e*.
- The comparative ending *-er* compares two things.
- The superlative ending *-est* compares more than two things.

PRACTICE Underline the *long-vowel spelling* in each word.

1. blaze

2. music

3. robot

4. bite

5. pilot

6. fume

7. major

8. stroke

Circle the *comparative* or *superlative adjective* in each sentence.

9. Is it safer to walk or ride a bike?

10. This salsa is the mildest one we have made.

11. Lola has the whitest smile.

12. Jake's dog is older than mine.

Copyright © McGraw-Hill Education. Permission is granted to reproduce for classroom use.

APPLY Circle the correct spelling of each word.
Write the correct spelling on the line.

13. unit   uneit   _____

14. wild   wiled   _____

15. blaed   blade   _____

16. cuteer   cuter   _____

17. zon   zone   _____

18. post   poste   _____

19. cradel   cradle   _____

20. boldest   boledest   _____

21. hive   hiv   _____

22. confus   confuse   _____

Copyright © McGraw-Hill Education. Permission is granted to reproduce for classroom use.

/n/ spelled *kn_* and *gn;* /r/ spelled *wr_*

FOCUS • The /n/ sound can be spelled with *kn_* and *gn.*
When using the letters *kn* or *gn* together, you
hear only the *n.*
• The /r/ sound can be spelled with *wr_.* When
using the letters *wr* together, you hear only
the *r.*

PRACTICE Add the letters as shown to form
a word. Write the word on the line, and then read
it aloud.

1. kn   +   ob   =   _____

2. gn   +   arl   =   _____

3. wr   +   inkle   =   _____

4. desi   +   gn   =   _____

5. kn   +   ife   =   _____

6. wr   +   ench   =   _____

Copyright © McGraw-Hill Education. Permission is granted to reproduce for classroom use.

APPLY Choose a word from the box to complete each sentence. Write the word on the line.

knelt	knack	wrap	gnat	wreck	knot	align	wrong

7. The string is tangled in a _____.

8. Braces help teeth _____ properly.

9. The catcher _____ in the dirt and waited for a pitch.

10. Mr. Miller lets us correct an answer if it is _____.

11. A _____ buzzed around the picnic table.

12. Thick fog caused the cars to _____.

13. I can help _____ the presents.

14. Amy is a singer with a _____ for high notes.

Copyright © McGraw-Hill Education. Permission is granted to reproduce for classroom use.

Vocabulary

Copyright © McGraw-Hill Education. Permission is granted to reproduce for classroom use.

> **FOCUS** Review the vocabulary words from "What Makes the Earth Shake?"

aloft	restless	secures	settled	shivers	spied

PRACTICE **Circle the letter that best answers each question below.**

1. Which is the best example of *spied*?

   a. a boy peeking through a window

   b. a boy who cannot sit still

2. Which is something that has *settled*?

   a. a sunken boat on the ocean floor

   b. a boat floating on the water

3. Which would a girl use if she *secures* her bike?

   a. She would use a bike lock.

   b. She would use a paintbrush.

4. Which is something that is held *aloft*?

   a. a flag folded in a drawer

   b. a flag flying at the top of a pole

Vocabulary

APPLY *Suffixes* are word endings that change the meanings of words. Read each sentence below. Circle the word that makes sense, based on what you know about each suffix and each vocabulary word.

Some Suffixes and Meanings

-ful = full of	*-y* = having or being
-less = without	*-er* = a person who does this
-ity = state or condition	

5. The tall, (lofty, settler) trees shaded the tiny house.

6. The (restless, restful) puppies would not sit still.

7. A (settler, security) is a person who moves to a new place.

8. The (shivery, lofty) children shook from the cold.

9. A quiet nap is a (restful, shivery) break.

10. The hug gave the child a feeling of (security, lofty).

Copyright © McGraw-Hill Education. Permission is granted to reproduce for classroom use.

Compare and Contrast

> **FOCUS**
> - To *compare* means to tell how things, events, or characters are alike. Some comparison clue words are *both, same, like,* and *too.*
> - To *contrast* means to tell how things, events, or characters are different. Some contrast clue words are *different, but,* and *unlike.*

PRACTICE Use the lines below to list details about an orange and a blueberry. Circle details they both share. Underline details that are different.

	Orange	Blueberry
Color	1. _____	4. _____
Shape	2. _____	5. _____
Size	3. _____	6. _____

Copyright © McGraw-Hill Education. Permission is granted to reproduce for classroom use.

Compare and Contrast

APPLY Read each paragraph. Then answer the questions comparing and contrasting the information.

Text 1: In an earthquake, you should do three things. The first is to drop onto your hands and knees. The second is to cover your head and neck by kneeling under a strong table. The third is to hold on until the shaking is over.

Text 2: It is never a good idea to try and move around during an earthquake. Studies have shown that people are much more likely to get hurt by a falling bookcase or lamp than from any other cause. Trying to get outside might seem smart, but it is safer to kneel under a strong table.

7. **Compare:** What do <u>both</u> texts say a person should do during an earthquake? _____

8. **Contrast:** What reasons does Text 2 give for staying put during an earthquake? _____

What reasons does Text 1 give for the steps it describes? _____

Access Complex Text • *Skills Practice 1*

Copyright © McGraw-Hill Education. Permission is granted to reproduce for classroom use.

Eliminating Irrelevant Information

Think

Audience: *Who* will read your writing?

_____

Purpose: *What* is your reason for writing about your topic?

_____

Practice

Read the paragraph below. Eliminate any irrelevant information by drawing a line through it.

Masked crabs are animals that use seaweed for protection. The crabs first tear the seaweed until it is soft. Seaweed is a type of water plant. Then the crabs put the seaweed on their bodies.

Masked crabs live in the North Atlantic, North Sea, and Mediterranean Sea. The Mediterranean Sea is big. Masked crabs walk backward to burrow in the sand. The crabs use their antennae to make a breathing tube.

The crabs have reddish brown and yellow colors. Blue is my favorite color. The crabs normally are about four centimeters long. The males are twice as big as the females. The crabs have four teeth. Two of their teeth are between their eyes.

Masked crabs like to eat worms and mollusks. These creatures are found where it is sandy. You can find dead masked crabs on the beach.

Copyright © McGraw-Hill Education. Permission is granted to reproduce for classroom use.

Revising

Use this checklist to revise your writing.

☐ Does your writing have a topic sentence?

☐ Does your writing include only facts and no opinions?

☐ Did you use language that makes your purpose clear to the reader?

☐ Did you include an ending that sums up your topic?

☐ Did you use words and phrases that present a neutral view?

Editing/Proofreading

Use this checklist to correct mistakes in your writing.

☐ Did you use proofreading symbols when editing?

☐ Did you use correct verb tenses?

☐ Do your sentences contain both subjects and predicates?

☐ Did you check your writing for spelling mistakes?

Publishing

Use this checklist to publish your writing.

☐ Write or type a neat copy of your writing.

☐ Add a photograph or a drawing.

Copyright © McGraw-Hill Education. Permission is granted to reproduce for classroom use.

/n/ spelled *kn_* and *gn*; /r/ spelled *wr_*; Comparative Ending *-er* and Superlative Ending *-est*

> **FOCUS**
> - Two ways /n/ can be spelled are *kn_* and *gn*.
> - One way /r/ can be spelled is *wr_*.
> - The **comparative ending** *-er* shows a comparison between two things. The ending *-er* is usually added to a base word.
> - The **superlative ending** *-est* shows a comparison between three or more things. The ending *-est* is usually added to a base word.

PRACTICE Sort the spelling words.

/n/ spelled *kn_*

1. _____

2. _____

/n/ spelled *gn*

3. _____

4. _____

/r/ spelled *wr_*

5. _____

6. _____

Comparative ending *-er*

7. _____

8. _____

Superlative ending *-est*

9. _____

10. _____

Word List		Challenge Words
1. wren	6. fastest	11. highest
2. knot	7. gnat	12. wrinkle
3. knife	8. sign	13. known
4. write	9. longer	14. looser
5. sharper	10. thickest	15. funniest

Copyright © McGraw-Hill Education. Permission is granted to reproduce for classroom use.

APPLY

**Circle the correct word to complete each sentence.
Write the correct spelling on the line.**

11. The cheetah is the (faster, fastest) animal on the savannah.

_____

12. A razor blade is (sharpest, sharper) than a pair of scissors.

_____

13. The (thicker, thickest) part of a tree trunk is usually near the ground. _____

14. *The Sound of Music* is a (longest, longer) film than *The Wizard of Oz*. _____

**Look at each word below. If the word is spelled
correctly, write "correct" on the line. If the word is
misspelled, write the correct spelling on the line.**

15. nat _____

16. rite _____

17. nife _____

18. ren _____

19. sine _____

20. knot _____

Copyright © McGraw-Hill Education. Permission is granted to reproduce for classroom use.

End Marks, Capitalization, and Proper Nouns

FOCUS
- Every sentence needs to end with punctuation, or an end mark.
- A **proper noun** names a specific person, place, or thing. A proper noun always begins with a capital letter.
  Example: Ethan is the nicest boy in **Adams Elementary School.**
- **Titles** in people's names begin with capital letters.
  Example: I have an appointment with **Dr.** Jilly.
- **Initials** from people's names are capitalized.
  Example: The author of *Stuart Little is* **E.B.** White.
- **Product names** begin with capital letters.
  Example: I bought a bag of **Salty's** pretzels.

PRACTICE **Triple-underline each proper noun, title, or set of initials that should be capitalized in the sentences below.**

1. John adams and John q. adams were presidents of the united states of america.

2. If the president of the united states is a man, then he is called mr. president.

3. Presidents t. roosevelt and franklin d. roosevelt were cousins.

Copyright © McGraw-Hill Education. Permission is granted to reproduce for classroom use.

APPLY Write the correct end mark at the end of each sentence.

4. Where does snow come from

5. Icy droplets of water in clouds turn into snowflakes

6. It is amazing that no two snowflakes are alike

7. Where do the water droplets come from

Write two sentences with product names in them. Be sure to capitalize the product names.

8. _____

9. _____

10. _____

Read the paragraphs below. Triple-underline the proper nouns, titles, and initials that should be capitalized.

The architect i. m. pei was born in china in 1917. mr. pei has designed many large, beautiful buildings. In the 1960s, he designed the terminal at jfk international airport in new york.

A landscape architect designs gardens and outdoor spaces. The first person to call himself a landscape architect was f. l. olmsted.

Copyright © McGraw-Hill Education. Permission is granted to reproduce for classroom use.

Grammar • *Skills Practice 1*

/ē/ spelled e and e_e

FOCUS The /ē/ sound can be spelled with e and e_e.

PRACTICE Read each sentence. Circle the word with /ē/. Write e or e_e on the line for the /ē/ spelling pattern of each word you circle.

1. Did you complete the chores? _____

2. Mom's present is a secret. _____

Choose a word from the box that makes sense in the sentence. Write the word on the line.

3. We _____ for math class after lunch.

Mr. Jones showed us a problem.

_____ helped us find the answer.

| before |
| He |
| began |

4. Jessica is a runner.

_____ wins a lot of races.

Jessica likes to _____.

| compete |
| rewind |
| She |

Copyright © McGraw-Hill Education. Permission is granted to reproduce for classroom use.

APPLY Look at the pairs of words below. Choose the correctly spelled word that will complete the sentence. Write the word on the line.

5. Gene is sick and has a _____.
   (fever, fevr)

6. An _____ is a person who plays sports.
   (athlet, athlete)

7. We will take a _____ before the lesson.
   (preetest, pretest)

8. _____ books belong to Lena.
   (These, Thes)

9. The sidewalk is made of _____.
   (concret, concrete)

10. Steve wants to _____ a doctor.
    (bee, be)

11. Two girls will _____ in the tennis match.
    (compete, compet)

12. The sign says "_____ of Dog!"
    (Bewear, Beware)

13. The Clarks will _____ their kitchen next spring.
    (reemodel, remodel)

14. Victor likes the school's new _____ song.
    (theme, them)

Copyright © McGraw-Hill Education. Permission is granted to reproduce for classroom use.

Review /ā/, /ī/, /ō/, /ū/, and /ē/

FOCUS
- The /ā/ sound can be spelled with *a* and *a_e*.
- The /ī/ sound can be spelled with *i* and *i_e*.
- The /ō/ sound can be spelled with *o* and *o_e*.
- The /ū/ sound can be spelled with *u* and *u_e*.
- The /ē/ sound can be spelled with *e* and *e_e*.

PRACTICE Use a word from the box to complete each sentence. Write the word on the line.

| brave | accuse | pride | tempo | find | delete | maple | robe |

1. Milo takes _____ in doing a good job.

2. The _____ tree is starting to lose its leaves.

3. The judge wore a black _____.

4. I can't _____ a pen in my backpack.

5. Did Jane _____ Pete of taking her paper?

6. Rachel was _____ when she saw the snake.

7. I like songs that have a fast _____.

8. It is wise to _____ old messages from your computer.

Copyright © McGraw-Hill Education. Permission is granted to reproduce for classroom use.

APPLY Unscramble the following letters and write each new word on the line. Underline the spelling pattern in each word.

9. z i e s _____

10. c o a n b _____

11. p s a e e t m d _____

12. e n m u _____

13. l a o t t _____

14. r d t a e _____

15. d i c l h _____

16. u e a s m _____

Write the long-vowel spelling for each word on the line.

17. Ohio _____

18. fume _____

19. hive _____

20. basic _____

21. precede _____

22. idol _____

Copyright © McGraw-Hill Education. Permission is granted to reproduce for classroom use.

Vocabulary

FOCUS Review the vocabulary words from "All about Earthquakes!"

absorb	boundaries	collide	energy	interact	plates	structures

PRACTICE Think about each underlined vocabulary word below. Match each item below with the best category name.

Item

1. a sponge

2. gasoline

3. a tall, steel skyscraper

4. a section of Earth's crust

Category

a. Strong Structures

b. Energy Sources

c. Earth's Tectonic Plates

d. Things That Absorb

Copyright © McGraw-Hill Education. Permission is granted to reproduce for classroom use.

Vocabulary

APPLY Read the sentences below. Write the vocabulary word that means the same thing as the underlined word or words.

5. _____ Most scientists think that long ago all of Earth's continents were one huge continent. This is called a supercontinent. <u>Huge parts of Earth's crust</u> are always on the move, though, so they began to move apart.

6. _____ Because of forces that made them <u>act on each other</u>, some plates turned or rotated.

7. _____ As they broke apart and moved, the <u>edges</u> of our modern continents came to be.

8. _____ How do scientists know this? They have studied <u>things that were built</u> inside certain kinds of rock.

9. _____ Some scientists think that far, far in the future, our continents will <u>crash into each other</u> again.

10. _____ The new landmass will <u>take in</u> all the old continents. There will be a supercontinent once more.

Copyright © McGraw-Hill Education. Permission is granted to reproduce for classroom use.

Name _____ **Date** _____

Cause and Effect

> **FOCUS**
> - A *cause* is why something happens.
> - An *effect* is what happens.

PRACTICE Read each *cause*, and write an *effect* to complete the sentence.

1. Since there was no rain, _____.

2. Because the volcano erupted, _____.

3. Because the farmer planted seeds, _____.

4. When the river overflowed its banks, _____.

5. Because an earthquake shook the abandoned shed, _____.

Copyright © McGraw-Hill Education. Permission is granted to reproduce for classroom use.

Cause and Effect

Look in "All about Earthquakes!" for the effects listed below. Then write a *cause* for each one.

6. **Effect:** A tsunami hits an area near shore.

   Cause: _____

7. **Effect:** Scientists closely watch plate movements.

   Cause: _____

8. **Effect:** The ground shakes.

   Cause: _____

Think about the following cause:

A family moves into a city where there are many earthquakes.

Write two effects.

9. _____

10. _____

Copyright © McGraw-Hill Education. Permission is granted to reproduce for classroom use.

Access Complex Text • *Skills Practice 1*

Name _____ Date _____

Writing to Inform

Think

Audience: *Who* will read your writing?

_____

_____

Purpose: *What* is your reason for writing about your topic?

_____

_____

Practice

Read each sentence below. If it uses formal language, write *F* on the line. If it uses informal language, write *I* on the line.

1. Bees are part of the ecosystem. _____

2. They play an important role in helping plants reproduce.
   _____

3. It's super cool how bees pollinate stuff. _____

4. Bees drink nectar from flowers. _____

5. When a bee lands on a flower, some of the pollen sticks to its body. _____

6. The bee zips over to the next flower, so he can chow down on more nectar. _____

Copyright © McGraw-Hill Education. Permission is granted to reproduce for classroom use.

Revising

Use this checklist to revise your writing.

☐ Does your writing have a topic sentence?

☐ Does your writing have facts that describe your topic?

☐ Did you define or explain words that a reader might not know?

☐ Did you use formal language?

Editing/Proofreading

Use this checklist to correct mistakes in your writing.

☐ Did you use proofreading symbols when editing?

☐ Did you use complete sentences?

☐ Did you use correct verb tenses?

☐ Did you check your writing for spelling mistakes?

Publishing

Use this checklist to publish your writing.

☐ Write or type a neat copy of your writing.

☐ Add a photograph or a drawing.

Copyright © McGraw-Hill Education. Permission is granted to reproduce for classroom use.

/ē/ spelled e and e_e; /ā/ spelled a and a_e; /ī/ spelled i and i_e; /ō/ spelled o and o_e; /ū/ spelled u and u_e

FOCUS
- Long vowels sound like their names.
- /ē/ can be spelled e and e_e.
- /ā/ can be spelled a and a_e.
- /ī/ can be spelled i and i_e.
- /ō/ can be spelled o and o_e.
- /ū/ can be spelled u and u_e.

PRACTICE Sort the spelling words.

/ē/ spelled e

1. _____

2. _____

/ē/ spelled e_e

3. _____

/ā/ spelled a

4. _____

/ā/ spelled a_e

5. _____

/ī/ spelled i

6. _____

/ī/ spelled i_e

7. _____

/ō/ spelled o

8. _____

/ō/ spelled o_e

9. _____

/ū/ spelled u_e

10. _____

Word List
1. label
2. vine
3. bonus
4. wild
5. begin
6. these
7. gate
8. use
9. meter
10. spoke

Challenge Words
11. basic
12. athlete
13. usual
14. equal
15. secret

Copyright © McGraw-Hill Education. Permission is granted to reproduce for classroom use.

APPLY

Write the spelling word that rhymes with each set of words below. The new word should have the same spelling pattern for the long-vowel sound.

11. mine   shine   _____

12. choke   broke   _____

13. mate   rate   _____

14. muse   fuse   _____

15. child   mild   _____

Write the correct spelling word on the line. Use the words from the box.

begin	label	these	bonus	meter

16. The DVD has several _____ features about the movie.

17. Use _____ markers because the other ones have dried out.

18. There is a gas _____ on the side of the building.

19. As soon as I get home from school, I _____ my homework.

20. Please check the _____ to see what size these shoes are.

Copyright © McGraw-Hill Education. Permission is granted to reproduce for classroom use.

Adjectives

> ***FOCUS*** • An **adjective** is a word that describes a noun.
> An adjective tells *how much, how many,* or
> *what kind*.
>
> **Examples:**
> • There are **five** classes of **living** things.
> • The **beautiful, pink** flower smelled **lovely**.
> • **Each** rabbit in the meadow is **furry**
>   and **brown**.

PRACTICE Read the poem below. Circle the adjectives.

For a big, green plant

Or a tiny, little ant

Resting in the quiet woods is nice.

For a tall oak tree

Or a busy, buzzing bee

Being in the bright sun is nice.

Each living thing must

Share cool shade and just

Take a long break in paradise.

Copyright © McGraw-Hill Education. Permission is granted to reproduce for classroom use.

APPLY Write two adjectives that could be used to describe each noun below.

1. apple _____   _____

2. sun _____   _____

3. cat _____   _____

4. jacket _____   _____

5. park _____   _____

Use the following adjectives in a sentence.

6. blue _____

7. confused _____

8. gentle _____

Read the paragraph below. Circle the adjectives.

Many creatures live in the forest. Blue birds and brown owls live in the forests. Red deer and gray squirrels live there too. Green frogs live in the forests that are near water. Sometimes a white rabbit can be found hopping through the thick forest. Have you ever seen a bear in the forest? I saw two bears yesterday.

Copyright © McGraw-Hill Education. Permission is granted to reproduce for classroom use.

/ē/ spelled *ee* and *ea*
Homographs and Homophones

> **FOCUS** The /ē/ sound can be spelled with ee and ea.

PRACTICE Read the words in the box aloud.
Then follow the directions below.

dream	week	feet	cheat

Write the words with /ē/ spelled like *leaf*.

1. _____   2. _____

Write the words with /ē/ spelled like *need*.

3. _____   4. _____

APPLY Write a word from the box to complete
each sentence.

5. Friday is the best day of the _____.

6. Reed's _____ is to become a pilot.

7. It is not fair to _____ on a test.

8. These socks keep Dena's _____ warm.

Copyright © McGraw-Hill Education. Permission is granted to reproduce for classroom use.

/ē/ Spelled e, ee, ea, e_e, y, ie • Homographs and Homophones

FOCUS
• **Homophones** are words that are pronounced the same, but they are spelled differently and have different meanings.
• **Homographs** are words that are spelled the same, but they have different meanings and sometimes different pronunciations.

FOCUS
• **Homophones** are words that are pronounced the same, but they are spelled differently and have different meanings. **Example:** *I can* <u>see</u> *a fish swimming in the* <u>sea</u>.

• **Homographs** are words that are spelled the same, but they have different meanings and sometimes different pronunciations.

PRACTICE Circle the correct *homophone* to complete each sentence.

9. The old steps (creek, creak) under my feet.

10. We all (past, passed) the test.

11. Hal was (find, fined) for parking in the wrong spot.

12. Mom helped me (reel, real) in the fish.

13. Did you (hear, here) the alarm ring?

14. Becca will (knead, need) a jacket for the trip.

APPLY Draw lines to connect each homograph to its meanings. Write the vowel sound the homograph makes on the line beside the correct definition.

15. _____ show the way; go first

16. _____ to wrap around   **a.** wind

17. _____ a type of metal

18. _____ a breeze   **b.** lead

Copyright © McGraw-Hill Education. Permission is granted to reproduce for classroom use.

/ē/ spelled ee, e_e, ea, and e

> **FOCUS** The /ē/ sound can be spelled with e, e_e, ee, and ea.

PRACTICE Underline the /ē/ spellings in the words below. Some words have two spellings for /ē/.

1. beagle
2. between
3. legal
4. seaweed
5. delete
6. complete
7. resubmit
8. extreme
9. reheat
10. depend

Copyright © McGraw-Hill Education. Permission is granted to reproduce for classroom use.

APPLY Choose the word that completes each sentence. Write the word on the line.

11. Eve wants a _____. But what does _____
    (tree, treat)   (she, me)

    _____ to eat? Will she have _____?
    (perfect, prefer)   (pants, peanuts)

    Or will she have something _____?
                                (sweet, sweat)

12. The talent show is only two _____ away.
                                  (weaks, weeks)

    Zeke can juggle _____ bags.
                     (been, bean)

    He also has a _____ puppet.
                   (zebra, zero)

    Zeke can _____ without moving his lips.
              (speck, speak)

    It _____ like the puppet talks!
        (seems, seams)

Copyright © McGraw-Hill Education. Permission is granted to reproduce for classroom use.

Vocabulary

> **FOCUS** Review the vocabulary words from "In My Own Backyard."

blurry	**haze**	**pulsed**	**sheets**
brook	**mist**	**settlers**	**skimmed**
grazed	**plowed**		

PRACTICE Write the vocabulary word that solves each riddle below. One riddle has two answers.

1. I am a cloud, a fog that can hide
   Anything that is lurking inside. _____ and _____

2. A farmer did this to get ready to sow
   Hundreds of seeds that will soon sprout and grow. _____

3. Your eyes are like this if you find that you need
   Glasses or contacts in order to read. _____

4. If cows did this, then on grass they did munch
   When roaming outside they decided to lunch. _____

5. People who first go over mountains or sand
   Are called this when once they stay in a new land. _____

Copyright © McGraw-Hill Education. Permission is granted to reproduce for classroom use.

Vocabulary

APPLY Read the definitions and the sentences below. Write the letter of the meaning that shows how the underlined word is used in each sentence.

sheet	**a.** A rectangle of cloth used on a bed.	**b.** A thin, broad piece or surface of something.

6. _____ The thin <u>sheet</u> of ice made the sidewalk slippery.

pulse	**a.** The regular throbbing of arteries caused by the heart beating.	**b.** To beat or vibrate.

7. _____ When the drums began to <u>pulse</u>, everyone danced.

8. _____ The runner felt his <u>pulse</u> to see how fast his heart was beating.

skim	**a.** To move over lightly.	**b.** To take a layer of something off a liquid.

9. _____ The insect could <u>skim</u> over the water because of surface tension.

10. _____ A cook will often <u>skim</u> fat off the top of broth.

brook	**a.** A small stream.	**b.** To put up with.

11. _____ "I will <u>brook</u> no rudeness!" the king shouted.

12. _____ The hikers crossed the <u>brook</u> in one easy jump.

Copyright © McGraw-Hill Education. Permission is granted to reproduce for classroom use.

Sequence

> ### FOCUS
> *Sequence* is the order in which events in a story occur. Writers often use time and order words to help readers understand the sequence of events.
>
> - *Time* words (*winter, today, night*) show the passage of time.
>
> - *Order* words (*first, next, finally*) show the order in which events happen.

PRACTICE Read the recipe below. Add order words from the box to complete the recipe.

finally	next	then	first

1. To make a small frittata, _____ break four eggs into a bowl and whisk them.

2. _____, add some shredded cheese.

3. _____ you might add small pieces of cooked vegetable.

4. _____ pour the mixture into a preheated nonstick skillet and cover.

5. _____ cook the top under a broiler, cool, and serve!

Copyright © McGraw-Hill Education. Permission is granted to reproduce for classroom use.

Sequence

APPLY A *timeline* shows ordered events from history.
Below is a timeline with some of the times the speaker saw.
Write events in time order in the blanks. (*Hint: Remember that
the speaker sees time going backward in the selection.*)

> Farm 100 years ago   Ice everywhere
> Dinosaurs grazing   Settlers and wagon

Giant dragonflies and huge trees

6. _____

Ancient camels and other mammals

People driving away a furry elephant

7. _____

Native Americans

8. _____

Workers at a sawmill

9. _____

Now, look at the selection's last page. Use the information
there, along with what you know, to decide what you think
would happen next if the story kept going.

10. _____

Copyright © McGraw-Hill Education. Permission is granted to reproduce for classroom use.

Name _____ Date _____

Writing to Inform
Think

Audience: *Who* will read your writing?

_____

Purpose: *What* is your reason for writing about
your topic?

_____

Prewriting

Use the idea web below to generate ideas about
adding visual elements to your writing.

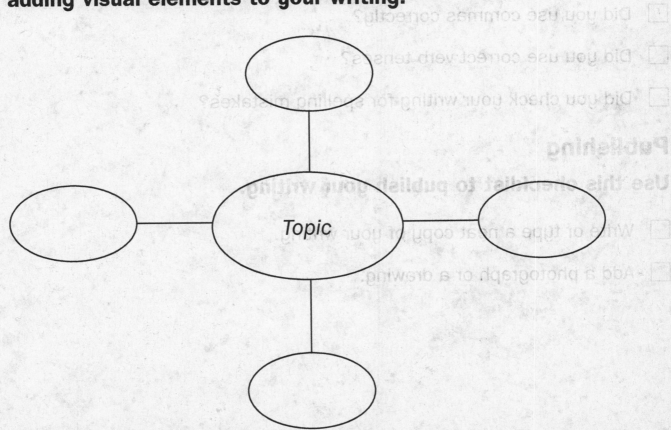

Topic

Copyright © McGraw-Hill Education. Permission is granted to reproduce for classroom use.

Revising

Use this checklist to revise your writing.

- ☐ Does your writing have a topic sentence?

- ☐ Does your writing include facts and explanations about the subject?

- ☐ Does your writing include place and location words?

- ☐ Did you use adjectives?

- ☐ Did you use words and phrases that show your point of view?

Editing/Proofreading

Use this checklist to correct mistakes in your writing.

- ☐ Did you indent the paragraph?

- ☐ Did you use proofreading symbols when editing?

- ☐ Did you use commas correctly?

- ☐ Did you use correct verb tenses?

- ☐ Did you check your writing for spelling mistakes?

Publishing

Use this checklist to publish your writing.

- ☐ Write or type a neat copy of your writing.

- ☐ Add a photograph or a drawing.

Copyright © McGraw-Hill Education. Permission is granted to reproduce for classroom use.

/ē/ spelled e, e_e, ee, and ea; Homophones

FOCUS
- /ē/ can be spelled e, e_e, ee, and ea.
- **Homophones** are words that are pronounced the same but have different spellings and meanings.

PRACTICE Sort the spelling words.

/ē/ spelled e

1. _____

/ē/ spelled e_e

2. _____

/ē/ spelled ee

3. _____

4. _____

5. _____

6. _____

7. _____

/ē/ spelled ea

8. _____

9. _____

10. _____

Word List		**Challenge Words**
1. real	6. steal	11. complete
2. sleep	7. creek	12. evening
3. we	8. creak	13. please
4. eve	9. knee	14. between
5. steel	10. reel	15. eagle

Copyright © McGraw-Hill Education. Permission is granted to reproduce for classroom use.

APPLY

Write the spelling words that correctly complete each pair of sentences below.

11. Homophones

The water in the _____ rose rapidly after it rained.

The rusty swing let out a loud _____ as Sam sat down.

12. Homophones

My dad bought me a new fishing _____.

These are _____ flowers, not plastic ones.

13. Homophones

The thief was caught red-handed trying to _____ the diamonds.

An ocean liner is made of _____, but it still floats.

Write the spelling word or words that rhyme with each word below.

14. jeep _____

15. steal _____

16. tree _____

17. weave _____

18. leak _____

Copyright © McGraw-Hill Education. Permission is granted to reproduce for classroom use.

Copyright © McGraw-Hill Education. Permission is granted to reproduce for classroom use.

Name _____ **Date** _____

Singular and Plural Nouns

FOCUS
- A **singular noun** names one of something.

  Examples: star, animal, plant, idea
- A **plural noun** names more than one of something.

  Examples: star**s**, animal**s**, plant**s**, idea**s**
- Most nouns add -s to make the plural form.

  Examples: car**s**, bike**s**, train**s**
- Nouns ending in *s, x, z, ss, ch,* or *sh* add **-es** to make the plural form.

  Examples: brush/brush**es**, box/box**es**
- Some nouns ending in *y* change the *y* to *i* before adding **-es.**

  Examples: budd**y**/budd**ies**, penn**y**/penn**ies**
- Some plural nouns do not follow a pattern.

  Examples: woman/**women**, sheep/**sheep**

PRACTICE Write the plural form of each noun below.

1. ax _____

2. rocket _____

3. sky _____

4. wish _____

5. goose _____

6. hoof _____

7. baby _____

8. person _____

APPLY Read the following sentences. Circle the plural nouns, and underline the singular nouns.

9. Different trees grow in different environments.

10. Fungi often grow near trees.

11. Branches often have leaves.

12. The wooden stem of a tree is called a trunk.

13. Geese gathered in the meadow with the sheep.

14. My new fish lives in my aquarium with my other fish.

15. Jake hurt his feet playing soccer.

16. What is your favorite flower?

Change the following nouns to plural and use them in a sentence

17. man _____

_____

18. ox _____

_____

19. child _____

_____

20. mouse _____

_____

Copyright © McGraw-Hill Education. Permission is granted to reproduce for classroom use.

Fluency Checklist

As you read the passage on the next page, be
sure to keep the following things in mind to help
you read with the appropriate rate, accuracy,
and expression.

As you read, make sure you

☐ pause longer at a period or other ending punctuation.

☐ raise your voice at a question mark.

☐ use expression when you come to an exclamation
point.

☐ pause at commas but not as long as you would at
a period.

☐ think of the character and how he or she might
say his or her words whenever you come to
quotation marks.

☐ remember not to read so fast that someone listening
cannot hear the individual words or make sense of
what is being read.

☐ stop and reread something that does not make sense.

Copyright © McGraw-Hill Education. Permission is granted to reproduce for classroom use.

A Wreck

Jean Smith just turned seven years old. A sign in her yard read, "Jean is seven!"

Jean's gift was a bike! It came in a huge box wrapped in white and green paper. Mom and Dad set the box in the yard. Jean knelt next to it and began to open it.

Jean was shocked! Jean did not see a bike. She just saw parts of a bike. She saw wheels and tires, green fenders, steel bars and pipes, knobs, pedals, and a seat. But she did not see a bike!

"That is not a bike!" Jean said. "It is a bike wreck!"

Both Mom and Dad chuckled. "No, it is not a wreck," said Mom.

"We just need to put these parts together." Dad added.

Mom held a paper that had been in the box. "We will read this. It will tell us how to do it," she told Jean.

After Mom read the paper, Mom and Dad got a wrench, a hammer, and other things. Jean helped Mom and Dad put the bike together. It did not take much time to finish.

The three Smiths looked at the green bike shining in the sun. "It looks pretty good for a wreck!" Dad said.

"I was wrong! It is not a wreck! It is my bike! I bet it is faster than most bikes!" Jean said.

Jean gave Mom and Dad a huge hug and said, "Thanks, Mom and Dad!"

Copyright © McGraw-Hill Education. Permission is granted to reproduce for classroom use.

Vocabulary

> **FOCUS** Review the vocabulary words from "Volcano Rising."

bulge	destructive	magma	streams
catastrophes	dome	majestic	swelling
creative	gases	seep	witness

PRACTICE *Antonyms* are words that mean the opposite or nearly the opposite of each other. Write a vocabulary word from the box that is an antonym for each word below.

seep	bulge	destructive
swelling	catastrophes	majestic

1. valley _____

2. creative _____

3. good fortune _____

4. humble _____

5. sinking _____

6. gush _____

Copyright © McGraw-Hill Education. Permission is granted to reproduce for classroom use.

Vocabulary

Apply Think about what you learned in "Volcano Rising." Complete each sentence below. Use at least one vocabulary word in each sentence completion.

gases	seep	creative
magma	streams	dome

7. Before lava comes erupting out of a volcano, _____.

8. When eruptions make new land, they are _____.

9. In an eruption, the air can be filled with _____.

10. When lava comes out of a volcano, it _____.

11. If there are cracks in a volcano, lava can _____.

12. When layers of lava cool, they form _____.

Copyright © McGraw-Hill Education. Permission is granted to reproduce for classroom use.

Main Idea and Details

FOCUS
- The *main idea* tells what a paragraph is about. It is the most important idea presented by the author.

- *Details* provide specific information about the *main idea*.

PRACTICE Read each paragraph. Draw a line under the main idea.

1. Volcanoes exist on other planets. The planet Venus is covered with volcanoes. Long ago volcanoes shaped Mercury, the planet closest to the sun. The largest volcano in our solar system is on the planet Mars and is 16 miles high.

2. There are several ways to classify volcanoes. Volcanoes can be active, which means they erupt regularly. Dormant volcanoes are quiet for now. Volcanoes can also be extinct, which means they will likely not erupt again.

3. Pumice is used in making concrete. Some people rub their skin with pumice to clear away rough patches. Pumice is used in making patterns on washed blue jeans. The volcanic rock pumice has many uses.

4. Volcanoes have many shapes. There are bulging domes. There are cone-shaped volcanoes. There are even wide, flat volcanoes.

Copyright © McGraw-Hill Education. Permission is granted to reproduce for classroom use.

Main Idea and Details

APPLY Think about what you learned from "Volcano Rising." Look at each group of details below. Write a main idea that could go with the details to form a paragraph.

5. Main Idea: _____

Details: Volcanoes help to build mountains. They create islands. They make new land.

6. Main Idea: _____

Details: Volcanoes can erupt underwater. They can form and erupt underneath glaciers. They can suddenly appear in the middle of a place where there were no volcanoes before.

Think about what you learned about earthquakes, volcanoes, and glaciers in Unit 2. Look at each main idea below. Use what you have learned to write two details to go with it.

7. Earth can change quickly. _____

_____

_____

8. Earth can change slowly. _____

_____

_____

Copyright © McGraw-Hill Education. Permission is granted to reproduce for classroom use.

Access Complex Text • *Skills Practice 1*

Name _____

/ā/ spelled *ai_* and *_ay*

> **FOCUS**
> - The /ā/ sound can be sp~~elled~~
> - Another letter follows the a~~i spelling~~
> - Another letter comes before ~~the ay~~

PRACTICE Read the words in the box a~~loud.~~

aim	paint	okay	display
rain	away	waist	maybe

Write the words with /ā/ spelled like *aid.*

1. _____   3. _____

2. _____   4. _____

Write the words with /ā/ spelled like *way.*

5. _____   7. _____

6. _____   8. _____

Copyright © McGraw-Hill Education. Permission is granted to reproduce for classroom use.

**... om the box to complete
the word on the line.**

braid	holiday	sway	explain
wait	spray	drain	maybe

9. Thanksgiving is my favorite _____.

10. Dana wears her hair in a _____.

11. The teacher will _____ our homework.

12. Nicole put _____ on her fishing hook.

13. Pull the plug to let the water _____ out of the sink.

14. Hank has to _____ for his turn on the swingset.

15. Keep the cat and dog _____ from each other.

16. _____ I will see you at the parade.

17. The tall trees _____ in the wind.

18. _____ the car with water to wash off all of the suds.

Copyright © McGraw-Hill Education. Permission is granted to reproduce for classroom use.

/ā/ spelled *a, a_e, ai_,* and *_ay*

> **FOCUS** The /ā/ sound can be spelled with *a, a_e, ai_,* and *_ay.*

PRACTICE Read the word in the box. Then read the sentence. Change the beginning of the word in the box to make a new rhyming word that completes the sentence.

1. | same | A wild animal is not _____.

2. | pay | Mixing black and white makes _____.

3. | fair | Shoes come as a _____.

4. | tray | The barn is filled with bales of _____.

5. | whale | The store is having a big _____.

6. | came | Write your _____ at the top of your paper.

7. | gain | Let's ride the _____ into the city.

8. | sway | We like to _____ kickball at the park.

9. | save | A big _____ crashed on the beach.

10. | stair | Pam likes to sit in the rocking _____.

Copyright © McGraw-Hill Education. Permission is granted to reproduce for classroom use.

APPLY Read each sentence. Circle the word that correctly completes the sentence.

11. James wants to _____ the leaves into a big pile.
    a. rake   **b.** rayke   **c.** rak   **d.** raik

12. If the _____ does not stop, we can play inside.
    a. raine   **b.** rane   **c.** rain   **d.** rayn

13. We made _____ pots in art class.
    a. claiy   **b.** clay   **c.** claye   **d.** clae

14. The _____ is locked each night at 9:00.
    a. gayt   **b.** gait   **c.** geyt   **d.** gate

15. Do you like red or green _____?
    a. grapes   **b.** graips   **c.** graypes   **d.** greyps

16. A monkey has a _____, but an ape does not.
    a. tayl   **b.** tael   **c.** taile   **d.** tail

17. Mother's Day is in the month of _____.
    a. Mai   **b.** Mae   **c.** May   **d.** Mey

18. A _____ of black horses pulled the wagon.
    a. payr   **b.** pair   **c.** pare   **d.** pear

19. We cannot _____ on the sidewalk.
    a. skat   **b.** skait   **c.** skate   **d.** skayt

20. Get a pump to _____ the flat tire.
    a. inflate   **b.** inflait   **c.** inflat   **d.** inflayt

Phonics • *Skills Practice 1*

Copyright © McGraw-Hill Education. Permission is granted to reproduce for classroom use.

Vocabulary

> **FOCUS** Review the vocabulary words from "Gross Jobs."

clogged	**expired**	**flexible**	**landfill**	**vital**
ensure	**flee**	**install**	**plant**	**waste**

PRACTICE **A simile compares two unlike things while using the word *like* or *as*. Circle the vocabulary word that completes each simile below.**

1. Your body is like a (plant, landfill) because it is an energy factory.

2. The children had to (flexible, flee) like rabbits because they realized they would be late.

3. The dancer was as (expired, flexible) as a thin wire.

4. The huge pile of (plant, waste) was like a mountain of trash.

5. The (vital, expired) milk was chunky like cottage cheese.

6. For Anna, reading was as (vital, installed) as breathing air.

Copyright © McGraw-Hill Education. Permission is granted to reproduce for classroom use.

Vocabulary

APPLY Select the correct vocabulary word to complete each sentence below.

install	ensure	vital
expired	clogged	landfill

7. Many people choose to _____ a disposal in their kitchen sink.

8. A disposal can grind up bits of old, _____ food.

9. This food would otherwise have just ended up in a _____.

10. To _____ that your disposal works well, do not put eggshells and large chunks of food in it.

11. If you pour fat down the drain, the disposal may become _____ with the fat.

12. Taking care of your disposal is _____ if you want it to last a long time.

Copyright © McGraw-Hill Education. Permission is granted to reproduce for classroom use.

Classify and Categorize

> ## FOCUS
> *Classifying* and *categorizing* help you organize information. It is a way of putting people, animals, and objects into different groups. It can help you see ways things are alike and different. It can also help you remember important ideas.

PRACTICE Think about what you learned from "Gross Jobs." Read each category title and items below. Circle the item that does *not* belong in each category.

1. **Plumber's Tools**

   a. plumber's snake   **b.** wrench   **c.** landfill

2. **Human Needs**

   a. food   **b.** television   **c.** shelter

3. **Risks of Pests in Homes**

   a. Pests can carry germs.

   b. Pests can live outside.

   c. Pests can bite.

4. **Reasons to Clean Out Your Refrigerator**

   a. Refrigerators are usually in kitchens.

   b. Food goes bad and smells.

   c. Expired food could make people sick.

Copyright © McGraw-Hill Education. Permission is granted to reproduce for classroom use.

Classify and Categorize

APPLY In "Gross Jobs," the author describes some jobs that can involve dirty work. Name two more jobs that could go in the category *Gross Jobs.* Explain your reasons for classifying them this way.

5. _____ belongs in this category because _____

_____.

6. _____ belongs in this category because _____

_____.

Think about the information in "Gross Jobs." Describe two tasks done by each of the following people:

A Janitor's Tasks

7. _____

8. _____

A Plumber's Tasks

9. _____

10. _____

Copyright © McGraw-Hill Education. Permission is granted to reproduce for classroom use.

Narrative Writing

Think

Audience: *Who* will read your writing?

_____

Purpose: *What* is your reason for writing your story?

_____

Prewriting

Use the spaces below to draw illustrations of four memories or ideas that could be used as the story in an action tale.

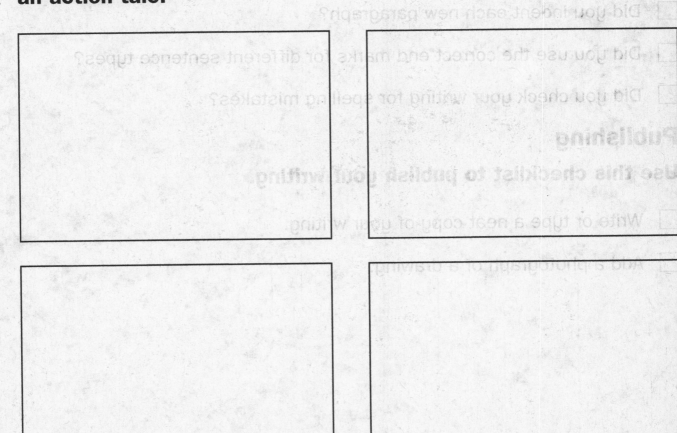

Copyright © McGraw-Hill Education. Permission is granted to reproduce for classroom use.

Revising

Use this checklist to revise your writing.

☐ Does your story have a strong beginning that introduces the main character?

☐ Does your story tell when and where it takes place?

☐ Did you use exciting and descriptive action verbs?

☐ Does the story have a strong ending?

☐ Does your writing have a clear purpose?

Editing/Proofreading

Use this checklist to correct mistakes in your writing.

☐ Did you use proofreading symbols when editing?

☐ Did you indent each new paragraph?

☐ Did you use the correct end marks for different sentence types?

☐ Did you check your writing for spelling mistakes?

Publishing

Use this checklist to publish your writing.

☐ Write or type a neat copy of your writing.

☐ Add a photograph or a drawing.

Copyright © McGraw-Hill Education. Permission is granted to reproduce for classroom use.

/ā/ spelled *ai_*, *_ay*, *a*, and *a_e*

FOCUS
- Long vowel *a* sounds like the letter *a*.
- Some ways the /ā/ sound can be spelled are *ai_*, *_ay*, *a*, and *a_e*.

PRACTICE Sort the spelling words.

/ā/ spelled *ai_*

1. _____
2. _____
3. _____

/ā/ spelled *_ay*

4. _____
5. _____
6. _____

/ā/ spelled *a*

7. _____
8. _____

/ā/ spelled *a_e*

9. _____
10. _____

Word List		Challenge Words
1. stay	**6.** chain	**11.** waist
2. rain	**7.** trace	**12.** railroad
3. base	**8.** play	**13.** pavement
4. April	**9.** paid	**14.** flavor
5. May	**10.** fable	**15.** Thursday

Copyright © McGraw-Hill Education. Permission is granted to reproduce for classroom use.

APPLY Write the spelling word that rhymes with each set of words below. The new word should have the same spelling pattern for the /ā/ sound.

11. day ray _____

12. cable stable _____

13. aid maid _____

14. chase case _____

15. main stain _____

Circle the misspelled words. Rewrite the words correctly below.

One of my favorite months is the month of Mai. In the month of Ayprul, there is always a lot of rayn, so you must plai indoors. In May, I like to do outdoor activities, such as making a daisy chane. I cannot wait for next May to come!

16. _____

17. _____

18. _____

19. _____

20. _____

Copyright © McGraw-Hill Education. Permission is granted to reproduce for classroom use.

Quotation Marks and Commas in Dialogue

FOCUS
- **Quotation marks** are placed before and after a speaker's exact words. They separate the spoken dialogue in a sentence from the words that describe who is speaking, or the tag.

- **Commas** also help separate the spoken dialogue from the tag. When the tag comes before the dialogue, then the comma comes before the opening quotation mark. When the tag comes after the dialogue, the comma comes before the closing quotation mark.
  Example: "The soccer team will practice at 3:30 today," said Ms. Childs.

PRACTICE Write *yes* or *no* to tell if the quotation marks and commas are used correctly or not.

1. "Look how much trash there is in the park said Olivia." _____

2. Luis said, "I think a lot of it blows here from other places." _____

3. "I have an idea!" exclaimed Olivia. _____

4. We should organize a clean-up day for the park," she explained. _____

APPLY Put quotation marks and commas where they are needed in these sentences.

5. Let's place a sign-up sheet in the classroom said Olivia.

6. Mr. Rickerts said I'll offer extra credit to anyone who helps.

7. The weather should be perfect on Saturday said Luis.

8. The park will look so much better! said Olivia.

9. Ethan asked What is the sign-up sheet for?

10. We are looking for volunteers to help clean the park said Mr. Rickerts.

Imagine talking with a friend about your favorite foods. Write the dialogue on the lines below. Be sure to use quotation marks and commas correctly.

_____

_____

_____

_____

_____

_____

_____

Copyright © McGraw-Hill Education. Permission is granted to reproduce for classroom use.

/ē/ spelled _ie_, _y, and _ey

> ## FOCUS
> - The /ē/ sound can be spelled with _ie_, _y, and _ey.
> - The _ie_ spelling pattern is usually found in the middle of a word.
> - The _y and _ey spelling patterns are usually found at the end of a word.

PRACTICE Read each word and underline the /ē/ spelling pattern.

1. shield

4. many

2. alley

5. valley

3. pretty

6. grief

Choose one of the /ē/ spelling patterns listed above to complete each word. Write the letter or letters to complete each word.

7. lad_____

10. y_____ld

8. ch_____f

11. cit_____

9. donk_____

12. barl_____

Copyright © McGraw-Hill Education. Permission is granted to reproduce for classroom use.

APPLY Read the sentence. Choose the word that
completes the sentence. Write the word on the line.

13. A _____ stole the gold ring.

(thief, thefe, theyfe)

14. My glass of milk is now _____.

(emptie, empty, emptee)

15. We watched the _____ swing on a rope.

(monkie, monkee, monkey)

16. Henry planted corn in the _____.

(feeld, field, feyld)

17. How much _____ is in the piggy bank?

(money, monie, mony)

18. Kathy felt _____ to win the raffle.

(lucky, luckie, luckey)

19. The _____ slept in her crib.

(babey, baby, babie)

20. Jerry likes _____ in his tea.

(honie, hony, honey)

21. Can you help me pick some _____ today?

(berrys, berries, bareys)

22. Will you read this _____ with me?

(storie, storey, story)

Copyright © McGraw-Hill Education. Permission is granted to reproduce for classroom use.

/ē/ spelled e, e_e, ee, ea, _ie_, _y, and _ey

> **FOCUS**
> • Long vowels sound like their names.
> • The /ē/ sound can be spelled with e, e_e, ee, ea, _ie_, _y, and _ey.

PRACTICE Unscramble the words below. Write the word on the first line and the /ē/ spelling pattern on the second line.

1. i d l f e _____ _____
2. e e n v _____ _____
3. z e e r e b _____ _____
4. y c z a r _____ _____
5. e r a h c _____ _____
6. y r l o l t e _____ _____
7. l d t e e e _____ _____
8. e e r f _____ _____
9. i o p s n e _____ _____
10. s y a e _____ _____

Copyright © McGraw-Hill Education. Permission is granted to reproduce for classroom use.

APPLY Circle the correct spelling for each word.

11. refund   reefund

12. finalley   finally

13. reason   reeson

14. cheif   chief

15. screan   screen

Choose a word from above to complete each sentence. Write the word on the line.

16. We looked for days and _____ found the lost ring.

17. The fire department promoted a new _____.

18. Did Julie give a _____ for being absent?

19. Please wipe the _____ with a soft cloth to keep it clean.

20. The store will _____ your money or let you make an exchange.

Copyright © McGraw-Hill Education. Permission is granted to reproduce for classroom use.

Vocabulary

> **FOCUS** Review the vocabulary words from "My Community and Me."

courteous	discover	fascination	relies	running
develop	evolve	gain	role	true

PRACTICE *Synonyms* mean the same or nearly the same thing. Match each vocabulary word with its synonym below.

1. develop   **a.** unfold

2. fascination   **b.** going

3. running   **c.** interest

4. courteous   **d.** polite

5. role   **e.** job

6. discover   **f.** obtain

7. relies   **g.** depends

8. gain   **h.** realize

Copyright © McGraw-Hill Education. Permission is granted to reproduce for classroom use.

Vocabulary

APPLY Use vocabulary words to complete the story below.

true	relies	gain
courteous	role	discover

The Plane Tree (a fable by Aesop)

Two men were walking in the hot sun. They came upon a large tree, so they sat under it.

One man looked up at the tree and saw it was a plane tree. "Plane trees are useless to our community," he said. "No one **9.** _____ on them for anything. What **10.** _____, or job, could they possibly have?"

The plane tree could have been angry, but instead it was gentle and **11.** _____ as it spoke. "Foolish man," the tree said. "If you thought for a minute, you would **12.** _____ my use. Isn't it **13.** _____ that when you sit under me, you **14.** _____ shade from the sun?"

Moral: A community's best blessings are often ignored.

Copyright © McGraw-Hill Education. Permission is granted to reproduce for classroom use.

Main Idea and Details

> ## FOCUS
> - The *main idea* tells what a paragraph is about. It is the most important idea presented by the author.
> - *Details* provide specific information about the *main idea*.

PRACTICE Each paragraph below is missing a main idea sentence. Circle the *main idea* that goes with each group of details.

1. Young babies cannot walk. They need someone to provide them with food and clothing.

   a. Young babies sleep a lot.

   b. Young babies need their parents.

2. Students discover ways to use numbers. They have a chance to read books and go on field trips.

   a. Students learn many new things at school.

   b. Communities have schools.

3. Communities often have police and fire stations. They might have public libraries and town halls.

   a. Communities have different kinds of public buildings.

   b. Police stations are busy places.

4. Good friends are good listeners. They spend time together.

   a. A good friend has many jobs.

   b. A good friend is hard to find.

Copyright © McGraw-Hill Education. Permission is granted to reproduce for classroom use.

Main Idea and Details

APPLY Think about what you learned from "My Community and Me." Look at each group of details below. Write a main idea that could go with the details to form a paragraph.

5. **Main Idea:** _____

Details: Being a good classmate means helping others. A good classmate listens when others speak. A good classmate asks others for help, too.

6. **Main Idea:** _____

Details: As you get older, you take on family responsibilities. You learn how to do jobs around the house. You no longer need your parents to help you as much.

Think about what you learned about community roles in "Gross Jobs" and "My Community and Me." Look at the main idea below. Use information from both selections to write two details to go with it.

Main Idea: People in a community depend on one another.

7. _____

_____

8. _____

_____

Access Complex Text • *Skills Practice 1*

Copyright © McGraw-Hill Education. Permission is granted to reproduce for classroom use.

Name _____ Date _____

Narrative Writing

Think

Audience: *Who* **will read your writing?**

_____

Purpose: *What* **is your reason for writing your story?**

_____

Prewriting

Use the story map below to plan your realistic story,
so the events are presented in a logical sequence.
Write the main events that will be told in the beginning,
middle, and end of your story.

Plot

Beginning (problem)	Middle (events)	Ending (how problem is solved)

Copyright © McGraw-Hill Education. Permission is granted to reproduce for classroom use.

Revising

Use this checklist to revise your writing.

☐ Does your story have a problem that must be solved?

☐ Does your story use temporal words to organize the events?

☐ Does your story have an ending that tells how the problem was solved?

☐ Did you include descriptive adjectives?

☐ Did you write using one point of view?

Editing/Proofreading

Use this checklist to correct mistakes in your writing.

☐ Did you use proofreading symbols when editing?

☐ Did you indent each new paragraph?

☐ Did you use adjectives and articles correctly?

☐ Did you correct any errors in point of view?

☐ Did you check your writing for spelling mistakes?

Publishing

Use this checklist to publish your writing.

☐ Write or type a neat copy of your writing.

☐ Add a photograph or a drawing.

Copyright © McGraw-Hill Education. Permission is granted to reproduce for classroom use.

/ē/ spelled _ie_, _y, _ey, ee, and ea

> **FOCUS**
> - Long vowels sound like their names.
> - The /ē/ sound can be spelled _ie_, _y, _ey, ee, and ea.

PRACTICE Sort the spelling words.

/ē/ spelled _ie_

1. _____

2. _____

/ē/ spelled _y

3. _____

4. _____

/ē/ spelled _ey

5. _____

6. _____

/ē/ spelled ee

7. _____

8. _____

/ē/ spelled ea

9. _____

10. _____

Word List

1. field
2. lady
3. money
4. breeze
5. stream
6. baby
7. speech
8. brief
9. monkey
10. teach

Challenge Words

11. squeeze
12. kneel
13. speaker
14. seashell
15. finally

Copyright © McGraw-Hill Education. Permission is granted to reproduce for classroom use.

APPLY Fill in the blank with a spelling word from the box.

| teach | money | stream | monkey | baby |

11. The small fish are swimming in the _____.

12. The _____ was swinging in a tree.

13. I asked my sister to _____ me how to ride a bike.

14. I gave my _____ to the cashier.

15. The _____ is ready for his bottle.

Circle the correct spelling for each word. Write the correctly spelled word on the line.

16. ladie   lady   _____

17. brief   breef   _____

18. breeze   breaze   _____

19. feyld   field   _____

20. speech   spiech   _____

Spelling • *Skills Practice 1*

Comparative Adjectives and Articles

> **FOCUS**
> - **Comparative adjectives** compare two nouns. The suffix **-er** is added to the end of an adjective to make it comparative.
> - **Superlative adjectives** compare three or more nouns. The suffix **-est** is added to the end of an adjective to make it a superlative adjective.
> - *A, an,* and *the* are **articles.** Articles are special types of adjectives.

PRACTICE Circle the comparative adjectives, superlative adjectives, or articles in the sentences.

1. Henry is taller than John, but Max is the tallest.

2. The quickest way to travel is by flying.

3. The play is tomorrow.

4. My mom's flowers are the prettiest in the neighborhood.

5. A full moon is brighter than a quarter moon.

Copyright © McGraw-Hill Education. Permission is granted to reproduce for classroom use.

APPLY Circle the correct word to complete each sentence.

6. You are the (luckier, **luckiest**) girl I know!

7. Mount Everest is the (higher, **highest**) mountain on Earth.

8. My dog barks (**louder**, loudest) than most other dogs.

9. The cat was fast, but the squirrel was (**faster**, fastest).

10. Hank was (**happier**, happiest) than his brother.

11. Turtles are often the (slower, **slowest**) animals in the forest.

12. The peacock's feathers were the (lovelier, **loveliest**) I've ever seen.

13. A golf ball is much (**smaller**, smallest) than a beach ball.

14. The (earlier, **earliest**) I have ever woken up is 4:00 in the morning.

Copyright © McGraw-Hill Education. Permission is granted to reproduce for classroom use.

/ā/ and /ē/ spellings

> **FOCUS**
> - The /ā/ sound can be spelled with *a*, *a_e*, *ai_*, and *_ay*.
> - The /ē/ sound can be spelled with *e*, *e_e*, *ee*, *ea*, *_ie_*, *_y*, and *_ey*.

PRACTICE Underline the /ā/ or /ē/ spelling pattern in each word. Write the pattern, and then write a new word that has the same spelling pattern. The words do not have to rhyme.

1. leap _____ _____

2. respond _____ _____

3. raise _____ _____

4. play _____ _____

5. athlete _____ _____

6. major _____ _____

7. flake _____ _____

8. bunnies _____ _____

9. jersey _____ _____

10. sweet _____ _____

Copyright © McGraw-Hill Education. Permission is granted to reproduce for classroom use.

APPLY Choose a word from the box to complete each sentence. Write the word on the line.

detail	squeaky	prepare	referee	daydream	shield

11. The shopping cart has a _____ wheel.

12. The _____ stopped the game due to rain.

13. A hat and glasses will _____ your face from the sun.

14. A story is more interesting with lots of _____.

15. When my mind wanders I _____ about the beach.

16. We begin to _____ dinner at 5:00.

Draw a line to connect the rhyming words.

17. played   delete

18. repeat   cheater

19. lazy   quirky

20. peeled   made

21. turkey   daisy

22. meter   yield

Copyright © McGraw-Hill Education. Permission is granted to reproduce for classroom use.

/f/ spelled *ph*, /m/ spelled _*mb*, and silent letters

> **FOCUS**
> - /f/ can be spelled with *ph*.
> - /m/ can be spelled with _*mb*. When using the letters *mb* together, the *b* is silent and you hear only the /m/ sound.
> - Silent letters in a word are not heard when the word is pronounced.

PRACTICE Add the letters shown to form a word. Write the word on the line, then read it aloud.

1. ph   +   oto   = _____

2. li   +   mb   = _____

3. co   +   mb   = _____

4. gra   +   ph   = _____

5. nu   +   mb   = _____

6. ph   +   ase   = _____

Read each word. Circle the letter or letters that are silent.

7. debt   **10.** character

8. hour   **11.** wrestle

9. science   **12.** adjust

Copyright © McGraw-Hill Education. Permission is granted to reproduce for classroom use.

APPLY Read the sentence. Choose the word that completes the sentence. Write the word on the line.

13. My _____ was ringing all day.

(fone, phone)

14. Maddie loves the _____ of this perfume.

(sent, scent)

15. Dad told us to _____ for the timer to beep.

(listen, lissen)

16. Mr. White called a _____ to fix the clogged drain.

(plumer, plumber)

17. A chart is made of rows and _____.

(columns, columbs)

18. Holly helped her little sister learn the _____.

(alphabet, alfabet)

19. A bridge connects the _____ to the mainland.

(iland, island)

20. Jonah pressed the button with his _____.

(thumb, thum)

21. A _____ makes a comparison between two things.

(metafor, metaphor)

22. Stephanie _____ up the ladder to the slide.

(climes, climbs)

Copyright © McGraw-Hill Education. Permission is granted to reproduce for classroom use.

Vocabulary

FOCUS Review the vocabulary words from
"Victor's Journal."

| blueprints | cement | frame | insulated | lever | while |

PRACTICE Decide whether the definition after each sentence gives the correct meaning of the underlined word in the sentence. Circle *Correct* or *Incorrect*.

1. The worker spread <u>cement</u> to create a new sidewalk.

Definition: "a powder mixed with water, rock, and sand to form concrete"
Correct   Incorrect

2. The architect created the <u>blueprints</u> for the new building.

Definition: "the skeleton of a building"
Correct   Incorrect

3. The builders <u>insulated</u> the walls of the house.

Definition: "covered with material that slows the flow of heat"
Correct   Incorrect

4. When the man pushed the <u>lever</u>, the machine turned on.

Definition: "a rod or bar that controls a machine"
Correct   Incorrect

Copyright © McGraw-Hill Education. Permission is granted to reproduce for classroom use.

Vocabulary

APPLY Use the vocabulary words to complete the
passage below.

| blueprints | cemented | frame | insulated | lever | while |

Inuit Houses

The Inuit people were the first settlers of the
country of Greenland. Because the north of Greenland
is so cold, Inuit sometimes built a type of house called
an igloo.

Many people think that the Inuit lived in igloos,
but that is not true. Inuit hunters only built igloos to
live in **5.** _____ they were far from the village.
Igloos were made out of large blocks of snow that were
6. _____ together when the ice melted and then
froze. Snow has pockets of air in it. Because of this,
the snow **7.** _____ the igloo and kept it warm
inside.

When Inuit people were not hunting, they lived
in either turf houses or tents. In the winter, the turf
houses, made of blocks of earth and stones, kept them
warm. In the warm summer months, Inuit people set up
tents. A typical Inuit tent had sealskin hides stretched
over a wooden **8.** _____.

Copyright © McGraw-Hill Education. Permission is granted to reproduce for classroom use.

Fact and Opinion

FOCUS • A *fact* states something that can happen, has happened, or is real. You can do research to check a fact.

• An *opinion* states something someone <u>believes</u> to have happened or to be true. Words often used in opinions include: *believe, think, feel, always, best, worst,* and *never.*

PRACTICE **Read each sentence below. Circle *Fact* or *Opinion*.**

1. The sun is a star.

        Fact   **Opinion**

2. I think everyone should learn to swim.

        Fact   **Opinion**

3. I believe that people will have flying cars someday.

        Fact   **Opinion**

4. A car is a type of vehicle.

        Fact   **Opinion**

5. Carrots are the best vegetable.

        Fact   **Opinion**

Copyright © McGraw-Hill Education. Permission is granted to reproduce for classroom use.

Fact and Opinion

APPLY Read the following quotes from "Victor's Journal." Decide if they are fact or opinion.

6. "A few months ago, the city placed a sign in the empty field across the street from my house."

   Fact or **Opinion**? _____

7. "I like to perform in plays, so I cannot wait!"

   Fact or **Opinion**? _____

8. "More than twelve builders started working before I left for school."

   Fact or **Opinion**? _____

9. "The panels looked like something from a science fiction movie!"

   Fact or **Opinion**? _____

Look at "Victor's Journal" and find the last entry with the title "Back to the *NEW* School." Find two facts and one opinion in this section. Write them on the lines below.

10. Fact: _____

11. Fact: _____

12. Opinion: _____

Access Complex Text • *Skills Practice 1*

Copyright © McGraw-Hill Education. Permission is granted to reproduce for classroom use.

Narrative Writing

Think

Audience: *Who* will read your writing?

_____

Purpose: *What* is your reason for writing your story?

_____

Practice

Action and describing words will make your personal narrative more interesting to read. Rewrite each sentence below using action and describing words. The first sentence has been completed as an example.

1. Ryan went up the stairs.

Example: Ryan **slowly crept** up the **creaky, wooden** stairs.

2. A bird flew.

_____

3. Ms. White drove her car.

_____

4. Emily got into the pool.

_____

Copyright © McGraw-Hill Education. Permission is granted to reproduce for classroom use.

Revising

Use this checklist to revise your writing.

☐ Does your story have a problem that is introduced at the beginning?

☐ Does your story make it clear to the reader when and where it takes place?

☐ Did you use action and describing words to make your writing more interesting?

☐ Does the story have a strong ending that tells how the problem was solved?

☐ Did you use first-person point of view?

Editing/Proofreading

Use this checklist to correct mistakes in your writing.

☐ Did you use proofreading symbols when editing?

☐ Did you use comparative and superlative adjectives correctly?

☐ Did you use commas correctly?

☐ Did you capitalize the beginnings of sentences and proper nouns?

☐ Did you check your writing for spelling mistakes?

Publishing

Use this checklist to publish your writing.

☐ Write or type a neat copy of your writing.

☐ Add a photograph or a drawing.

Copyright © McGraw-Hill Education. Permission is granted to reproduce for classroom use.

/f/ spelled *ph*; /m/ spelled *_mb*; Silent Letters

FOCUS
- One way the /f/ sound can be spelled is *ph*.
- One way the /m/ sound can be spelled is *_mb*.
- Some words contain silent letters. These letters are not heard when the word is said.

PRACTICE Sort the spelling words.

/f/ spelled *ph*

1. _____

2. _____

3. _____

/m/ spelled *_mb*

4. _____

5. _____

6. _____

Silent letter *b*

7. _____

Silent letter *h*

8. _____

Silent letter *l*

9. _____

Silent letter *c*

10. _____

Word List		Challenge Words
1. limb	**6.** graph	**11.** alphabet
2. herb	**7.** half	**12.** island
3. lamb	**8.** scent	**13.** plumber
4. doubt	**9.** phase	**14.** nephew
5. phone	**10.** comb	**15.** photo

APPLY Circle the correct spelling for each word.
Write the correct spelling on the line.

11. The (cent, scent) of baking bread drifted from the kitchen.

_____

12. A (lam, lamb) stood quietly with the rest of the sheep.

_____

13. When the (fone, phone) rang, my mother answered it.

_____

14. The barber used a (come, comb) to hold up her hair.

_____

**Look at each word below. If the word is spelled
correctly, write "correct" on the line. If the word is
misspelled, write the correct spelling on the line.**

15. phase _____

16. erb _____

17. libm _____

18. graf _____

19. doubt _____

20. half _____

Copyright © McGraw-Hill Education. Permission is granted to reproduce for classroom use.

Capitalization—Days, Months, Holidays, Cities and States

> **FOCUS**
> - Calendars will help you remember to capitalize the **days** of the week, the **months** of the year, and **holidays.**
> - You must also capitalize the names of **cities** and **states.** Names of specific **rivers**, **lakes**, and **mountains** should also be capitalized.

PRACTICE Write the name of the day or month on the line to complete each sentence below.

1. The day before Wednesday is _____.

2. The first day of January we celebrate
_____.

3. The last day of the year is in _____.

4. The day before Friday is _____.

5. We celebrate our nation's birth on _____.

6. The day after Friday is _____.

Copyright © McGraw-Hill Education. Permission is granted to reproduce for classroom use.

APPLY Read the poem. Triple-underline each letter that should be capitalized.

Thirty days has september,

april, june, and november;

All the rest have thirty-one.

february has twenty-eight alone;

save in leap year, at which time,

february's days are twenty-nine.

Read the paragraph. Triple-underline each letter that should be capitalized.

My class was studying unusual names of cities in the United States. I began my report on february 28, 2015. I read about boulder, colorado. I wonder if the rocks in that city are bigger than the rocks in little rock, arkansas. Do buffaloes really live in buffalo, new york? Does everyone sew in needles, california? I finished my report on march 6, 2015.

Read the paragraph. Triple-underline each letter that should be capitalized.

The rappahannock river is located in virginia. It is the longest free-flowing river in the eastern united states. It is also a tidal river. The blue ridge moutains are to the west of it. It enters the chesapeake bay, south of the potomac river. The chesapeake bay is near the atlantic ocean. The river goes through fredericksburg, virginia, an important historical city.

Copyright © McGraw-Hill Education. Permission is granted to reproduce for classroom use.

/s/ spelled ce, *ci_*, and *cy*

> **FOCUS** The /s/ sound can be spelled *ce*, *ci_*, and *cy*.

PRACTICE Read each word aloud. Underline the spelling pattern that makes /s/ sound.

1. ice

2. policy

3. pencil

4. center

5. lacy

6. city

7. trace

8. civil

Use a word from the box to complete each sentence. Write the word on the line.

rice	circus	fancy	fleece

9. Clowns make people happy at the _____.

10. Let's eat at a _____ restaurant on your birthday.

11. Grace wore her _____ coat to practice.

12. The beans and _____ taste good!

Copyright © McGraw-Hill Education. Permission is granted to reproduce for classroom use.

APPLY Choose a word from the box that makes sense in the sentence. Write the word on the line.

13. We went out to eat dinner.

The pizza was in the shape

of a _____.

I ate three _____.

| circle |
| fancy |
| slices |

14. Jack's _____ loves

to read. Her favorite subject

is _____.

| percent |
| science |
| niece |

15. Rebecca's family lives in

the _____. When they need

_____ to run, they go

to the park.

| city |
| race |
| space |

16. Cole cannot _____

on his work. He is _____

about going to Ellen's party.

| concern |
| concentrate |
| excited |

Copyright © McGraw-Hill Education. Permission is granted to reproduce for classroom use.

/j/ spelled *ge* and *gi_*

FOCUS The /j/ sound can be spelled *ge* and *gi_*.

PRACTICE Read each word aloud. Underline the spelling pattern that makes the /j/ sound.

1. rage

2. logic

3. giant

4. gentle

5. cringe

6. giraffe

7. orange

8. general

Read the words in the box. Write each word under the correct heading.

digest	frigid	tragic	twinge	general	ginger

ge	*gi_*
9. _____	12. _____
10. _____	13. _____
11. _____	14. _____

Copyright © McGraw-Hill Education. Permission is granted to reproduce for classroom use.

APPLY Read the sentence. Choose the word that correctly completes the sentence. Write the word on the line.

15. Angela left a _____ for you.
(message, messig)

16. The car's _____ needs a tune-up.
(enjine, engine)

17. The number 153 has three _____.
(digits, digets)

18. Can you _____ what it's like to be a bird?
(imagen, imagine)

19. We stayed in a _____ by the lake.
(cottage, cottij)

20. Be very _____ with the bunnies.
(gintle, gentle)

21. The glass vase is quite _____.
(fragel, fragile)

22. Let's plant a _____ garden.
(vegetable, vegitable)

23. Marge ordered a _____ beverage.
(larj, large)

24. The cash _____ prints our receipt.
(register, regester)

Phonics • *Skills Practice 1*

Copyright © McGraw-Hill Education. Permission is granted to reproduce for classroom use.

Vocabulary

FOCUS Review the vocabulary words from
"The Langston Times."

blared	officials	result	seams	sources
features	progress	revealing	solar panels	values

PRACTICE Match each vocabulary word with its example below.

1. officials   **a.** sewn edges of a coat

2. solar panels   **b.** large panels that capture energy from sunlight

3. sources   **c.** the money gold and silver are worth

4. values   **d.** opening a present

5. revealing   **e.** places where rivers begin

6. result   **f.** the outcome of an experiment

7. seams   **g.** the details of what a new computer can do

8. features   **h.** leaders of a town

Copyright © McGraw-Hill Education. Permission is granted to reproduce for classroom use.

Vocabulary

APPLY *Synonyms* mean the same or nearly the same thing. Write the vocabulary word that is a synonym for each underlined word below.

blared	officials	result	seams	sources
features	progress	revealing	solar panels	values

9. The family was making good <u>headway</u> cleaning out the house, so they decided to have a garage sale.

_____

10. Nadia had the job of writing the <u>worth</u> of each item on a piece of paper. _____

11. Jamaal created a series of tables <u>displaying</u> the items for sale in an exciting way.

_____

12. They <u>blasted</u> music while they set up, but turned the volume down once customers started arriving.

_____

13. Nadia had written <u>details</u> about the more expensive items so people would know what they were buying.

_____

14. She also let people know <u>origins</u> of the special items.

_____

15. The <u>outcome</u> of their hard work was a great garage sale.

_____

Copyright © McGraw-Hill Education. Permission is granted to reproduce for classroom use.

Compare and Contrast

> ## FOCUS
> - To *compare* means to tell how things, events, or characters are alike. Some comparison clue words are *both, same, like,* and *too.*
> - To *contrast* means to tell how things, events, or characters are different. Some contrast clue words are *different, but,* and *unlike.*

PRACTICE Circle whether the sentence is *comparing* or *contrasting*. Then write the clue word on the line.

1. Cement trucks and dump trucks are both types of construction equipment.

   compare   **contrast**   _____

2. A soccer field and a baseball field are both near the new school.

   compare   **contrast**   _____

3. People have used electricity for a while, but solar panels are a recent source.

   compare   **contrast**   _____

4. The old building used to be big enough, but now is too small.

   compare   **contrast**   _____

Copyright © McGraw-Hill Education. Permission is granted to reproduce for classroom use.

Compare and Contrast

APPLY Look again at "The Langston Times."
Read the following details about the old school.

Langston Elementary School's old building did not have a cafeteria, so students had to eat lunch in their classrooms. There was a small field outside but no playground equipment. People had talked of making a school garden, but the lot did not have space for one. Some classes had to meet in trailers because the building was too small.

Now contrast details of the new and old buildings. Write four sentences telling how they are different.

5. _____

6. _____

7. _____

8. _____

Copyright © McGraw-Hill Education. Permission is granted to reproduce for classroom use.

Narrative Writing

Think

Audience: *Who* will read your fantasy?

_____

Purpose: *What* is your reason for writing your fantasy?

_____

Prewriting

Use the story map below to plan your fantasy story,
so the events are presented in a logical sequence.
Write the main events that will be told in the
beginning, middle, and end of your story.

Plot

Beginning (problem)	Middle (events)	Ending (how problem is solved)

Copyright © McGraw-Hill Education. Permission is granted to reproduce for classroom use.

Proofreading Symbols

¶   Indent the paragraph.

^   Add something.

℘   Take out something.

/   Make a small letter.

≡   Make a capital letter.

sp   Check spelling.

⊙   Add a period.

Copyright © McGraw-Hill Education. Permission is granted to reproduce for classroom use.

/s/ spelled ce, *ci_*, and *cy*; /j/ spelled ge and *gi_*

> **FOCUS**
> - Three ways /s/ can be spelled are ce, *ci_*, and *cy*.
> - Two ways /j/ can be spelled are ge and *gi_*.

PRACTICE Sort the spelling words.

/s/ spelled ce

1. _____

2. _____

3. _____

/s/ spelled *ci_*

4. _____

5. _____

/s/ spelled *cy*

6. _____

/j/ spelled ge

7. _____

8. _____

9. _____

/j/ spelled *gi_*

10. _____

Word List		Challenge Words
1. age	6. spicy	11. piece
2. peace	7. face	12. gentle
3. pencil	8. gem	13. tragic
4. magic	9. circus	14. century
5. ice	10. large	15. excite

Copyright © McGraw-Hill Education. Permission is granted to reproduce for classroom use.

APPLY Write the correct spelling word next to its meaning clue.

11. something you write with _____

12. a feeling of calm and quiet _____

13. frozen water _____

14. how old someone is _____

Circle the correct spelling for each spelling word. Write the correct spelling on the line.

15. majic   magic   _____

16. serkus   circus   _____

17. face   fase   _____

18. spisee   spicy   _____

19. large   larj   _____

20. jem   gem   _____

Copyright © McGraw-Hill Education. Permission is granted to reproduce for classroom use.

Colons and Commas—Items in a Series

FOCUS
- A **comma** is used after each item in a series or list of things, except after the last item.
- A **colon** can be used in a sentence to introduce a list.
  Example: The following items may be brought to camp: a backpack, a sleeping bag, and a flashlight.
- A **colon** is also used to separate the hours and minutes when writing time.
  Example: Your piano lesson is postponed until 4:30 today.

PRACTICE Commas and colons have been left out of the sentences below. Put commas and colons where they are needed.

1. Fleas flies and bees drive me crazy!

2. Insects eat some of the following things wood paper and even other insects.

3. Bats birds and reptiles also eat insects.

4. At 10 30 every morning, I eat a red juicy and tasty apple.

5. Cars can be red blue black or green.

6. These are the colors on the Italian flag red white and green.

Copyright © McGraw-Hill Education. Permission is granted to reproduce for classroom use.

APPLY Write a list of items for each topic.

Favorite Foods

7. _____

8. _____

9. _____

Favorite Pets

10. _____

11. _____

12. _____

Write a sentence about each topic. Include your list as a series of items, and use commas correctly.

13. _____

_____

14. _____

_____

Read the story, and add commas where they are needed. Use proofreading symbols.

Flowers have soft petals pretty colors and a nice smell. To grow flowers, you must plant the seeds water the plants and pull the weeds. Flowers look pretty in a garden in your office or in your house. Today we will plant purple pansies white daisies and lilies all around the border of the garden.

Copyright © McGraw-Hill Education. Permission is granted to reproduce for classroom use.

/ī/ spelled _igh, _ie, and _y

> **FOCUS** The /ī/ sound can be spelled _igh, _ie, and _y.

PRACTICE Unscramble the following words. Write the word on the first line and the /ī/ spelling on the second line.

1. k y s _____ _____

2. r i f e d _____ _____

3. g t h i t _____ _____

4. s i s p e _____ _____

5. l e t s y _____ _____

Write three sentences using the words above.

6. _____

_____

7. _____

_____

8. _____

_____

Copyright © McGraw-Hill Education. Permission is granted to reproduce for classroom use.

APPLY Choose a word from the box to complete each sentence. Write the word on the line.

bright	lie	why	type	might	applied

9. If you sleep in, you _____ miss the bus.

10. _____ is the alarm ringing?

11. Lilah wore a _____ yellow rain jacket.

12. Brian _____ for a job at the market.

13. Telling a _____ is not a way to solve problems.

14. What _____ of pet is your favorite?

Draw a line matching a word on the left to a rhyming word on the right.

15. try   **a.** high

16. night   **b.** fight

17. sighs   **c.** dry

18. pie   **d.** dries

Copyright © McGraw-Hill Education. Permission is granted to reproduce for classroom use.

/ī/ spelled *i, i_e, _igh, _ie,* and *_y*

FOCUS The /ī/ sound can be spelled *i, i_e, _igh, _ie,* and *_y.*

PRACTICE Underline the /ī/ spelling pattern in each of the following words.

1. idea

5. light

2. criticize

6. incline

3. flies

7. China

4. title

8. shy

Change the first letter or letters of each word to make a new rhyming word. Write the word on the line.

9. bride _____

10. kind _____

11. child _____

12. flight _____

13. tie _____

14. by _____

Copyright © McGraw-Hill Education. Permission is granted to reproduce for classroom use.

APPLY Choose a word from the box to complete each sentence. Write the word on the line.

high	beside	diet	quiet	prize
unties	shiny	why	trial	advice

15. We must be _____ in the library.

16. Bo won the _____ for best costume.

17. Is the top shelf too _____ for you to reach?

18. Jess is on a dairy-free _____.

19. _____ do you like pizza so much?

20. Whenever I need help, Uncle Hal always gives me really good _____.

21. Mark always _____ his shoes before he takes them off.

22. The twins like to sit _____ each other.

23. The judge wore a black robe during the _____.

24. Sally polished the car until it was _____.

Copyright © McGraw-Hill Education. Permission is granted to reproduce for classroom use.

Vocabulary

> **FOCUS** Review the vocabulary words from "The Stranger and the Soup."

gasp	plaza	sighed	surely	wilted
indeed	seasoning	simmer	well	wringing

PRACTICE Antonyms mean the opposite or nearly the opposite. Circle the vocabulary word that means the opposite of each word or phrase below.

1. perked up   *wilted* or *sighed*

2. not really   *indeed* or *wringing*

3. freeze   *seasoning* or *simmer*

4. unsteadily   *sighed* or *surely*

Write the vocabulary word that matches each clue below.

5. I am a place where people gather in the middle of a town.

_____

6. I am a place where people can fill a bucket with water.

_____

Copyright © McGraw-Hill Education. Permission is granted to reproduce for classroom use.

Vocabulary

APPLY Use the vocabulary words to complete the story below.

gasp	plaza	sighed	surely	wilted
indeed	seasoning	simmer	well	wringing

Tricky Spider and Turtle

One day Spider had Turtle over for dinner. Spider
7. _____ greens and added lots of wonderful
8. _____. The food smelled wonderful! It smelled so
good that Spider did not want to share it.

"Before you eat," Spider told Turtle, "you need to
wash your dirty feet." Turtle let out a **9.** _____ when
he saw how dirty his feet were, and ran out to wash
them. By the time he came back in, Spider had eaten
all the food.

A few weeks later, Turtle had Spider over for dinner.
Turtle lived under the water at the bottom of a
10. _____. "You are **11.** _____ welcome," called
Turtle to Spider. "Come to my table!"

Spider tried to swim down, but he was too light. He
12. _____ in frustration. Then he had the idea of
putting stones in his coat pockets. Now Spider sank to
the table.

"Excuse me," said Turtle, "but it is bad manners to
wear your coat at the dinner table."

Spider took off his coat. Slowly but **13.** _____,
he floated back up to the surface. He floated,
14. _____ his hands in frustration as Turtle ate the
dinner.

Copyright © McGraw-Hill Education. Permission is granted to reproduce for classroom use.

Making Inferences

> ### FOCUS
> When you *make inferences*, you use information provided in a text, along with what you already know, to understand details the author did not put in the story.

PRACTICE Read each group of sentences. Circle the correct *inference*.

1. The grass was soaking wet. Beads of water dripped slowly off the bike the child had left out in the yard overnight.

   a. It was a warm fall day.

   b. It had rained during the night.

2. The shirt was very clean. It had a tag hanging from one sleeve. It did not have any wrinkles.

   a. The shirt was new.

   b. The shirt needed to be washed.

3. The boy whispered something to his mother. His mother laughed.

   a. The boy told a joke to his mother.

   b. The mother did not hear the boy.

4. The cat looked at the bowl of food. It walked away.

   a. The cat was very hungry.   **b.** The cat was full.

Copyright © McGraw-Hill Education. Permission is granted to reproduce for classroom use.

Making Inferences

APPLY Read each quote from "The Stranger and the Soup." Use what you already know to answer each question that follows and make an inference.

"He was dressed in a long cape with a hood and carried a walking stick. He moved slowly but surely down the road that led to Isabel's village."

5. What inference can you make about what this stranger is doing?

_____

_____

6. What information did you use to make this inference?

_____

_____

"And sure enough, the stranger gave a knock at Isabel's door. Her mother opened it just wide enough to stick out her head. 'What is the meaning of this?' she asked."

7. What inference can you make about how Isabel's mother felt toward the stranger?

_____

_____

8. What information did you use to make this inference?

_____

_____

Copyright © McGraw-Hill Education. Permission is granted to reproduce for classroom use.

Using Action and Describing Words

Practice

Use action and describing words to fill in the blanks in the sentences below.

1. Troy and his _____ dog went for a(n) _____ walk today.

2. In the middle of the walk, something _____ happened.

3. Troy's dog Buster talked very _____.

4. Buster told Troy about a _____ field where there was a spaceship.

5. Buster and Troy _____ to the field.

6. They were playing on the spaceship when the spaceship _____ _____ _____ _____.

Apply

Use the lines below to list action and descriptive words that you could use in your fantasy.

_____ _____

_____ _____

_____ _____

Copyright © McGraw-Hill Education. Permission is granted to reproduce for classroom use.

Revising

Use this checklist to revise your writing.

☐ Does your story include elements of fantasy?

☐ Does your story make it clear to the reader when and where it takes place?

☐ Did you use action and describing words to make your writing more interesting?

☐ Did you use temporal words to show the reader the sequence of events?

☐ Does your story have a beginning, middle, or ending?

Editing/Proofreading

Use this checklist to correct mistakes in your writing.

☐ Did you use proofreading symbols when editing?

☐ Did you correct any sentence problems, such as fragments or run-on sentences?

☐ Do all of your sentences have subject/verb agreement?

☐ Did you use quotation marks and commas correctly in dialogue?

☐ Did you check your writing for spelling mistakes?

Publishing

Use this checklist to publish your writing.

☐ Write or type a neat copy of your writing.

☐ Add a photograph or a drawing.

Copyright © McGraw-Hill Education. Permission is granted to reproduce for classroom use.

/ī/ spelled _igh, _y, _ie, i, and i_e

> **FOCUS**
> - Long vowels sound like their names.
> - The /ī/ sound can be spelled _igh, _y, _ie, i, and i_e.

PRACTICE Sort the spelling words.

/ī/ spelled _igh

1. _____

2. _____

/ī/ spelled _y

3. _____

4. _____

5. _____

/ī/ spelled _ie

6. _____

7. _____

/ī/ spelled i

8. _____

/ī/ spelled i_e

9. _____

10. _____

Word List		Challenge Words
1. pie	6. right	11. recognize
2. night	7. shy	12. skyscraper
3. fly	8. lie	13. style
4. pile	9. mice	14. knight
5. child	10. try	15. mighty

Copyright © McGraw-Hill Education. Permission is granted to reproduce for classroom use.

APPLY Write the spelling word or words that rhyme with each set of words below. The new word will have the same /ī/ spelling pattern. The first one is done for you.

11. tie   die   pie   lie

12. cry   dry   _____   _____

13. dice   twice   _____

14. flight   might   _____   _____

15. file   mile   _____

Circle the correct spelling for each word. Write the correct spelling on the line.

16. nyte   night   _____

17. child   chield   _____

18. mighce   mice   _____

19. pie   py   _____

20. try   trie   _____

Copyright © McGraw-Hill Education. Permission is granted to reproduce for classroom use.

Name _____ **Date** _____

Subject/Verb Agreement

FOCUS A sentence must have a **subject** and a **verb** that agree. This means the subject and the verb must both be singular, or they must both be plural.

- If the subject of a sentence is singular, the verb must be singular.
- If the subject of a sentence is plural, the verb must be plural.

PRACTICE Write *S* if the sentence has a singular subject and verb. Write *P* if the sentence has a plural subject and verb.

1. Many plants can be kept inside to grow. _____

2. Herbs are plants used in cooking. _____

3. A wildflower grows by itself outside. _____

4. An evergreen tree keeps its leaves all year long. _____

5. An oak tree loses its leaves in the fall. _____

6. Palm trees love the hot sun. _____

Copyright © McGraw-Hill Education. Permission is granted to reproduce for classroom use.

APPLY Write *am*, *is*, or *are* on the line to agree with the subject in each sentence.

7. We _____ learning about plants and trees.

8. A tree _____ a type of plant.

9. I _____ enjoying these lessons.

Write *have* or *has* on the line to agree with the subject in each sentence.

10. Evergreens _____ leaves or needles.

11. The desert _____ many plants.

In the sentences below, choose the verb in parentheses ( ) that correctly completes each sentence.

12. Benji (rake, rakes) the leaves in our yard in autumn.

13. The leaves (changes, change) color from green to brown, yellow, and orange.

14. We (have, has) a great time jumping in piles of leaves.

Copyright © McGraw-Hill Education. Permission is granted to reproduce for classroom use.

A Rainy Day

Rain fell again. Mike told Mom, "This is so much rain! It has been raining day and night."

"Well, farm fields need rain. Rain will help my garden," said Mom.

"But, Mom, this much rain is boring!" said Mike.

For a while, Mike played different kinds of games on Mom's laptop in the den. But that quickly felt boring, as well. Then Mike just looked out at the yard. He gazed at the gray sky. The rain had stopped a bit. Now there was even a gopher on top of the fence. How did it climb up there?

Then Mike gazed at the street. Thanks to the rain, there was a tiny stream of water running down the side of the cement curb. The water rushed to a rusty drain. Mike saw the stream carry leaves down the street. Most leaves fell in the drain. Only some leaves did not. Why did those leaves escape the drain?

Before he realized it, Mike was thinking about what it might be like to ride a leaf on the current. If he were tiny like a leaf, could he slide over that drain and not drop in?

Copyright © McGraw-Hill Education. Permission is granted to reproduce for classroom use.

Mike pretended he sat on the center of a leaf. He tightly held its edges while it spun around in the rushing stream. Mike twisted his body left and right. He tried to control the leaf! He had to lead it around wide gaps in the drain! He was not afraid. "I believe I can do it," Mike said to himself.

Soon Mike felt wet and cold! Fresh rain hit his face. He felt water rush over his leaf's edges!

Suddenly, the giant drain was right there! With great skill, Mike turned his leaf this way and that. Would the leaf fall into the drain's gaps? Or would Mike safely lead his leaf past those gaps?

Look out! Mike came close to slipping off his leaf! As he hung on, it spun and spun. Oh no! But Mike's leaf spun past the drain's gaps! It was not easy, but Mike made it! He was safe! As his leaf glided gently down the street, Mike yelled, "Yes!"

Mom came into the den. "Mike, did that yell mean rain is not boring?" she asked.

Mike grinned and said, "No, Mom. It means my daydreams are not boring!"

Copyright © McGraw-Hill Education. Permission is granted to reproduce for classroom use.

Vocabulary

FOCUS Review the vocabulary words from "Night Shift."

adjust	lingers	perishable
assemble	maneuverable	port
freight	nocturnal	shift
jam	nudges	smartly

PRACTICE Match each word with its definition.

1. port

2. nudges

3. smartly

4. adjust

5. freight

6. nocturnal

7. maneuverable

8. lingers

9. perishable

10. jam

a. capable of being moved easily

b. goods carried by ships or trucks

c. active at night

d. staying on as time passes

e. gently pushes

f. neatly

g. likely to spoil quickly

h. something that wedges

i. place where boats can dock

j. to change so as to correct

Copyright © McGraw-Hill Education. Permission is granted to reproduce for classroom use.

APPLY **Read the definitions and the sentences below. Write the letter of the meaning that shows how the underlined word is used in each sentence.**

assemble	**a.**	To put together.
	b.	To gather together in a place.

11. _____ The family chose to <u>assemble</u> for a reunion.

jam	**a.**	A sweet spread made of fruit.
	b.	Something that blocks or wedges.

12. _____ The girl tried to fix the paper <u>jam</u> in the printer.

13. _____ The sandwich had peanut butter and <u>jam</u> on it.

shift	**a.**	A small change in position.
	b.	A time during which a worker has a job to do.

14. _____ The security guard ended his <u>shift</u> and went home.

15. _____ The sailor felt the winds <u>shift</u> and change.

Copyright © McGraw-Hill Education. Permission is granted to reproduce for classroom use.

Vocabulary • *Skills Practice 1*

Cause and Effect

FOCUS
- A *cause* is why something happens.
- An *effect* is what happens.

PRACTICE Read each cause, and write an effect to complete the sentence.

1. Because it rained on the family's camping trip,

_____

2. Because the girl was just learning to roller skate,

_____

3. When the boy dropped the china plate,

_____

4. Since the car was out of gas,

_____

5. Because the man works at night,

_____

Copyright © McGraw-Hill Education. Permission is granted to reproduce for classroom use.

APPLY Look in "Night Shift" for the effects listed below. Then write a cause for each one.

6. **Effect:** Paint splatters a car on the bridge.

   Cause: _____

7. **Effect:** The security guard turns down the radio and checks all the doors and windows.

   Cause: _____

8. **Effect:** The truck driver is stuck in a traffic jam.

   Cause: _____

Think about the following cause:

People are hungry when they are working the night shift.

Write two effects based on events and information in "Night Shift."

9. _____

10. _____

Access Complex Text • *Skills Practice 1*

Copyright © McGraw-Hill Education. Permission is granted to reproduce for classroom use.

Graphic Organizer Resources

Name _____ Date _____

Cause and Effect

Cause

Effect

Cause

Effect

Copyright © McGraw-Hill Education. Permission is granted to reproduce for classroom use.

Compare and Contrast

Different

Same

Different

Copyright © McGraw-Hill Education. Permission is granted to reproduce for classroom use.

Name _____ **Date** _____

Sequence

First

[box]

Next

[box]

Last

[box]

Copyright © McGraw-Hill Education. Permission is granted to reproduce for classroom use.

Fact and Opinion

Fact	Opinion

Copyright © McGraw-Hill Education. Permission is granted to reproduce for classroom use.

Name _____ Date _____

Date _____

Making Inferences

Inference

=

Prior Knowledge

+

Clue

Copyright © McGraw-Hill Education. Permission is granted to reproduce for classroom use.

Story Map

Beginning

Middle

Ending

Copyright © McGraw-Hill Education. Permission is granted to reproduce for classroom use.

Word Map 1

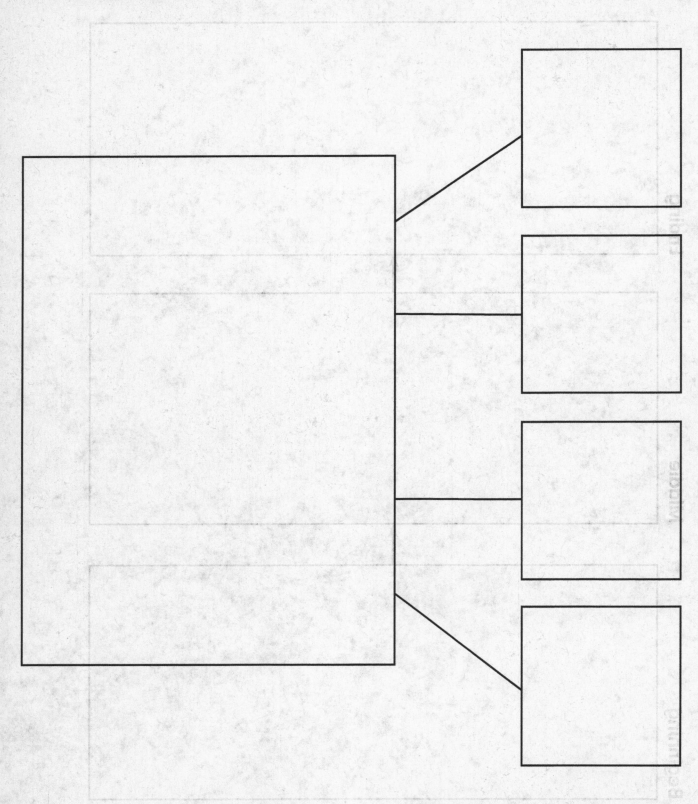

Copyright © McGraw-Hill Education. Permission is granted to reproduce for classroom use.

Word Map 2

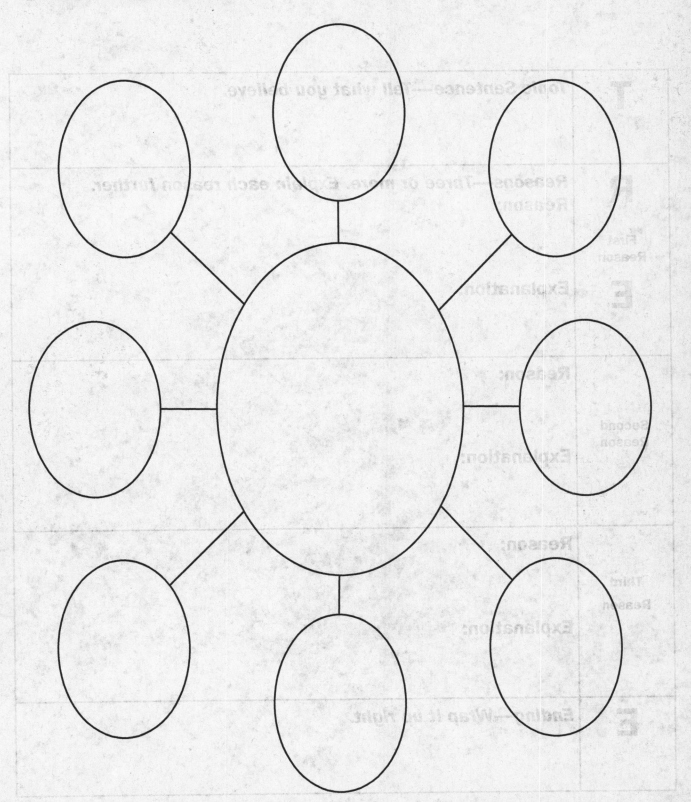

Copyright © McGraw-Hill Education. Permission is granted to reproduce for classroom use.

TREE

T	*Topic Sentence—Tell what you believe.*	
R **First Reason** **E**	*Reasons—Three or more. Explain each reason further.* **Reason:** **Explanation:**	
Second Reason	**Reason:** **Explanation:**	
Third Reason	**Reason:** **Explanation:**	
E	*Ending—Wrap it up right.*	

Copyright © McGraw-Hill Education. Permission is granted to reproduce for classroom use.

WWW-H2-W2

W	**W**ho are the characters in the story?
W	**W**hen does the story take place?
W	**W**here does the story take place?
H	**H**ow do the characters react at different points in the story?
H	**H**ow does the story end?
W	**W**hat does the main character want to do?
W	**W**hat happens in the story?

Copyright © McGraw-Hill Education. Permission is granted to reproduce for classroom use.

Idea Web

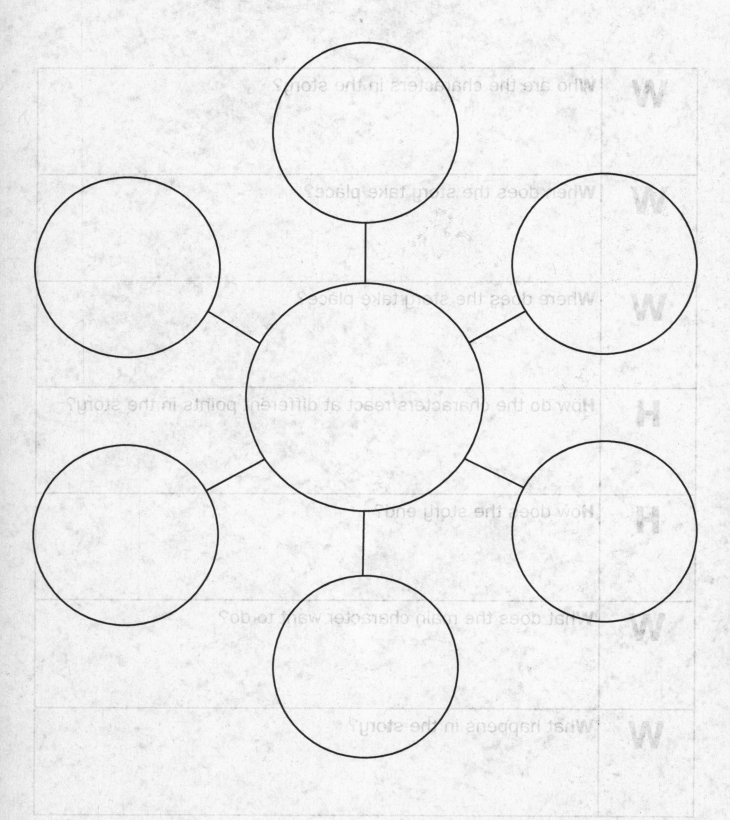

Copyright © McGraw-Hill Education. Permission is granted to reproduce for classroom use.

Answer Key

Unit 1, Lesson 1 • *Pages 1–2*
1–3. /ch/: chap, pinch, chat
4–6. /th/: thump, with, thorn
7–9. / sh/: rash, shot, fish
10. ship
11. moth
12. thud
13. trash
14. chest
15. inch
16. shed
17. champ
18. slush
19. lunch
20. with

Unit 1, Lesson 1 • *Pages 3–4*
1. scarf
2. which
3. dark
4. whip
5. when
6. market
7. where
8. wham
9. whiff
10. what
11. dart
12. spark/parks
13. garden
14. charm
15. barn
16. sharp/harps
17. hard
18. yarn/nary
19. start/tarts
20. radar

Unit 1, Lesson 1 • *Pages 5–6*
1. observed
2. safety
3. shelter
4. admired
5. merchant
6. platform
7. safety
8. huddled

9. b
10. b

Unit 1, Lesson 1 • *Pages 7–8*
1. **Effect:** The mice needed a new home. **Cause:** The shoe had holes in it.
2. **Effect:** Pa had money to buy tools. **Cause:** Pa sold their broken furniture.
3. **Effect:** The family stayed dry. **Cause:** The new house had a roof.

Possible Answers: 4–6
4. a boy knocked the lamp over.
5. he did not put on sunscreen.
6. people drank all the water.
7. The cat put his paw in the shoe.
8. The mice family had built a house.

Unit 1, Lesson 1 • *Pages 9–10*
Audience: a teacher or other students
Purpose: to share my opinion
Prewriting Possible Answers:
1. Otters are the best animals at the zoo.
2. Kids should go to school only four days a week.
3. The Exploratorium is great place.
4. Everyone should know how to ride a bike.
5. All cars should run on electricity.
6. Everyone should plant a tree.

Unit 1, Lesson 1 • *Pages 11–12*
1. chin
2. march
3. which
4. chop

5. ship
6. shed
7. harsh
8. shark
9. march
10. harsh
11. shark
12. that
13. with
14. which
15. shark
16. harsh
17. that
18. chin
19. ship
20. chop
21. with
22. which
23. shed
24. march

Unit 1, Lesson 1 • *Pages 13–14*
Practice:
1. Mrs. Smith
2. Allison
3. Riverside Hospital.
4. class, fish
5. things
6. glasses
Apply:
Proper nouns: Melissa, Goshen Lane Elementary School, Mr. Sanchez, Hilary, Tuesday
Common nouns: name, student, second grade, teacher, friend, teacher, recess, afternoon, class, school, place, things, friends
7. **Possible Answer:** Nicole
8. **Possible Answer:** Atlanta
9. **Possible Answer:** Roosevelt Elementary School
10. **Possible Answer:** Ms. Young

Copyright © McGraw-Hill Education. Permission is granted to reproduce for classroom use.

Answer Key

Unit 1, Lesson 2 • *Pages 15–16*
1. pep/per
2. pic/nic
3. ex/pand
4. hic/cup
5. shel/ter
6. tun/nel
7. tab/let
8. cob/web
9. bas/ket
10. man/tel
11. rab/bit
12. lap/top
13. clas/sic
14. tem/per
15. slip/per

Possible Answers: 16–20
16. Mom asked me to dust the mantel.
17. This song is a classic.
18. I got in trouble for my bad temper.
19. I found my slipper under my bed.
20. I have a rabbit background on my laptop.

Unit 1, Lesson 2 • *Pages 17–18*
1. tch, a
2. ck, a
3. ck, i
4. dge, i
5. tch, a
6. dge, e
7. tch
8. ck
9. dge
10. tch
11. dge
12. ck
13. nudge
14. pitcher
15. locker
16. track
17. stretch
18. bridge

Unit 1, Lesson 2 • *Pages 19–20*
1. Yes
2. No
3. Yes
4. Yes
5. No
6. shelter
7. liquid
8. predators
9. honeydew
10. scurry

Unit 1, Lesson 2 • *Pages 21–22*
1. contrast, but
2. compare, both
3. contrast, different
4. contrast, unlike

Possible Answers: 5–6
5. Scales and aphids both make honeydew.
6. Aphids suck juices from garden plants, while scales suck juices from trees.

Unit 1, Lesson 2 • *Pages 23–24*
Audience: a teacher or other students
Purpose: to share my opinion
Prewriting Possible Answers:
1. **Reason #1:** It is a big place.
   Explanation #1: You won't feel cooped up.
   Additional Detail: One area is as big as a football field.
2. **Reason #2:** There are many things to do.
   Explanation #2: You won't get bored.
   Additional Detail: aquarium, science demonstrations

3. **Reason #3:** It is educational.
   Explanation #3: You can have fun and learn at the same time.
   Additional Detail: They teach about gravity, animals, and Earth.

Unit 1, Lesson 2 • *Pages 25–26*
1. wedge
2. judge
3. ledge
4. badge
5. check
6. kick
7. track
8. flock
9. latch
10. switch
11. kick
12. flock
13. wedge
14. judge
15. watch
16. switch
17. badge
18. track
19. latch
20. ledge

Unit 1, Lesson 2 • *Pages 27–28*
Practice:
1. play
2. saw
3. wanted
4. fixed
5. planted
6. cleaned
7. said
8. make

Copyright © McGraw-Hill Education. Permission is granted to reproduce for classroom use.

Answer Key

Apply:
It is important for every person to <u>recycle</u>. You can <u>help</u> Earth and <u>save</u> energy. You can <u>sort</u> trash at home into paper, plastic, and metal containers. New things can be <u>made</u> from these used items. People can also <u>use</u> things in different ways instead of <u>putting</u> them in the trash. For example, <u>pack</u> your lunch in a reusable bag. You can also <u>take</u> a cloth bag to the grocery store. There are many ways to <u>love</u> Earth. The first Earth Day <u>happened</u> in 1970. Every year on April 22, people <u>do</u> things to <u>help</u> Earth. We should <u>make</u> every day Earth Day.

Unit 1, Lesson 3 • *Pages 29–30*
1. brushes
2. boxes
3. wishes
4. paths
5. classes
6. charts
7. champs
8. suffixes
9. sharks
10. hills
11. foxes
12. branches
Possible Answers: 13–16
13. The lifeguard spotted sharks near the coast.
14. We look for bike paths with lots of hills.
15. There are foxes in the forest.
16. The tree branches are bare during the winter.

Unit 1, Lesson 3 • *Pages 31–32*
1. dodged
2. blossomed
3. stretched
4. planned
5. instructed
6. shrugged
7. tricked
8. clapped
9. pledged
10. expanded
11. patched
12. pledged
13. patched
14. tricked
15. clapped
16. expanded

Unit 1, Lesson 3 • *Pages 33–34*
1. b
2. a
3. c
4. c
5. a
6. emphasize
7. loyal
8. accepted
Possible Answers: 9–10
9. my birthday dinner.
10. to exercise daily.

Unit 1, Lesson 3 • *Pages 35–36*
Possible Answers: 1–12
1. strawberries
2. apples
3. pears
4. broccoli
5. carrots
6. spinach
7. dog, lion
8. canary, robin
9. Bat
10. Bat tried to trick the Beasts by hiding his wings.
11. Ox

12. Ox is a member of the Beasts team, and the story said the Beasts are big and strong.

Unit 1, Lesson 3 • *Pages 37–38*
Audience: a teacher or other students
Purpose: to share my opinion
Prewriting Possible Answers:
Opinion: Plant a tree.
Reason: Trees are beautiful.
Reason: Trees release oxygen.
Reason: Trees are homes to animals.
Reason: Trees clean the air.

Unit 1, Lesson 3 • *Pages 39–40*
1. shops
2. stacks
3. patches
4. wishes
5. pitches
6. clapped
7. locked
8. picked
9. started
10. grabbed
11. shops
12. patches
13. stacks
14. wishes
15. pitches
16. grabbed
17. locked
18. started
19. picked
20. clapped

Unit 1, Lesson 3 • *Pages 41–42*
Practice:
1. H
2. H
3. L
4. L
5. H

Copyright © McGraw-Hill Education. Permission is granted to reproduce for classroom use.

Answer Key

Apply:
Linking Verbs: are, is, are, was
Helping Verbs: have, have, have, have
There <u>are</u> six fish swimming in my aquarium. The blue fish <u>was/is</u> swimming faster than the orange fish. My cat <u>was/is</u> watching them swim. I <u>have</u> tried to teach the cat to behave. These fish <u>are</u> not for dinner, Miss Kitty! For dinner you <u>will</u> have cat food.

Unit 1, Lesson 4 • *Pages 43–44*
1–3 /ng/: rang, hung, king
4–6 /nk/: honk, shrunk, tank
7. drinking
8. strumming
9. nudging
10. jogging
11. blending
12. swinging
13. link
14. banging
15. long
16. crank
17. chunk
18. winking

Unit 1, Lesson 4 • *Pages 45–46*
1. gar/gle
2. pan/el
3. met/al
4. freck/le
5. an/vil
6. shriv/el
7. shuf/fle
8. fos/sil
9. ras/cal
10. sten/cil

11. rental
12. tranquil
13. model
14. puddle
15. gravel
16. sparkle
17. novel
18. lentil
19. apple
20. animal

Unit 1, Lesson 4 • *Pages 47–48*
1. b
2. d
3. a
4. e
5. c
6. b
7. a
8. c
9. furious
10. part
11. pity
12. roared
13. humbly
14. disappointed

Unit 1, Lesson 4 • *Pages 49–50*
1. 1; Yesterday
2. 5; Finally
3. 2; First
4. 3; Next
5. 4; hour
6. 6; After
7. The hero of the game would be a famous warrior.
8. First the ball was tossed.
9. Next, Flying Bat got the ball from Big Bear.
10. Finally, Flying Bat scored.
11. Flying Bat went to live in a cave.
Possible Answer: 12
12. Flying Bat was a hero, but I think he stayed away, alone in the cave, because he was humble.

Unit 1, Lesson 4 • *Pages 51–52*
Audience: a teacher or other students
Purpose: to share my opinion
Prewriting Possible Answers
Topic: Animals
Opinion 1: Giraffes are interesting.
Opinion 2: Animals in zoos should not be in cages.
Opinion 3: Everyone should put up a bat house.

Unit 1, Lesson 4 • *Pages 53–54*
1. strong
2. middle
3. pickle
4. gravel
5. think
6. shrank
7. blank
8. sink
9. rushing
10. grinning
11. think
12. strong
13. gravel
14. middle
15. blank
16. rushing
17. sink
18. pickle
19. shrank
20. grinning

Unit 1, Lesson 4 • *Pages 55–56*
Practice:
1. **Subject:** Soccer;
   Predicate: began in England in the 1800s.
2. **Subject:** Two teams of eleven players each;
   Predicate: compete in soccer.

Copyright © McGraw-Hill Education. Permission is granted to reproduce for classroom use.

Skills Practice 1

Answer Key

3. **Subject:** The players;
   Predicate: try to put a ball into the other team's goal.
4. **Subject:** The goals;
   Predicate: are two nets at opposite ends of a rectangular field.
5. **Subject:** Each goal;
   Predicate: is worth one point to the team that scored.

Apply:

6. S
7. P
8. P
9. S
10. P
11. S
12. S

Possible Answers:

13. **Subject:** My volleyball team
    Predicate: won the big game.
14. **Subject:** We
    Predicate: will be going to the fair.
15. **Subject:** Summer vacation
    Predicate: is almost here.

Unit 1, Lesson 5 • *Pages 57–58*

1–2 *er:* verb, buzzer
3–4 *ir:* shirt, girl
5–6 *ur:* slurp, turnip
7–8 *ear:* heard, earn
9. ur
10. ir
11. er
12. er
13. ear
14. ur
15. turning
16. sister's
17. Stir
18. earn, dollars

Unit 1, Lesson 5 • *Pages 59-60*

1. bore
2. store
3. pore
4. tore
5. core
6. border
7. story
8. portal
9. torn
10. corn
11. wore
12. fork
13. short
14. adore
15. horse
16. cord—**d.** bored
17. form—**b.** storm
18. forecast—**e.** contrast
19. support—**c.** escort
20. shore—**a.** chore

Unit 1, Lesson 5 • *Pages 61–62*

1. c
2. e
3. g
4. h
5. f
6. d
7. b
8. a
9. check

Possible Answer: 10
10. checking
11. manage
Possible Answer: 12
12. management
13. pierce
Possible Answer: 14
14. pierced
15. eager
Possible Answer: 16
16. eagerly

Unit 1, Lesson 5 • *Pages 63-64*

1. a
2. a
3. b

Possible Answers: 4–8

4. I can infer that Danny really loves his brother.

5. The text talks about him jumping out of bed and his heart leaping.
6. I know that when I feel that way about someone visiting, I really care about that person.
7. Bob and the coach are disappointed.
8. The text describes them as shaking their heads.

Unit 1, Lesson 5 • *Pages 65–66*
Audience: a teacher or other student
Purpose: to share my opinion
Prewriting Possible Answers:
Topic: Bats
Positive words
helpful
unique
amazing
Negative words
ugly
scary
pest

Unit 1, Lesson 5 • *Pages 67-68*

1. antlers
2. perched
3. bird
4. whirling
5. purple
6. short
7. stork
8. chores
9. snored
10. explore
11. short
12. bird
13. snored
14. whirling
15. chores
16. perched
17. purple
18. explore

Copyright © McGraw-Hill Education. Permission is granted to reproduce for classroom use.

Answer Key

19. stork
20. antlers

Unit 1, Lesson 5 • *Pages 69–70*
Practice:

Did you know that the teddy bear is over one hundred years old? This popular toy has been around longer than the electric light, telephone, and motor car. In 1902, President Theodore Roosevelt was on a hunting trip and had the chance to shoot a captured bear. He refused, saying "Spare the bear!" A cartoon was drawn of this event and put in the newspaper. Two shopkeepers, Morris and Rose Michtom, made a soft bear, which they called Teddy's Bear. The teddy bear was an overnight success and is still very popular today.

Apply:
Possible Answers:

My favorite toys are Hot Wheels. There are so many different kinds of cars. The tracks are also fun. My favorite car is red with blue stripes. It is very fast.

Dear Lucas,

I had a great time visiting you. It was fun to play video games and ride our bikes. Your sister, Amelia, was fun too. Next time maybe we can go in your tree fort. Please tell your mom thank you for letting me come to visit.

Sincerely,
Noah

Unit 1, Lesson 6 • *Pages 73–74*
1. journey
2. entire
3. panic
4. face
5. surface
6. slick
7. raged
8. It means you take it on as your own.
9. It will go faster.
10. You clean it well.
11. You are surprised.
12. The weather changed.

Unit 1, Lesson 6 • *Pages 75–76*
1. a
2. a
Possible Answers: 3–8
3. Pam ran over to Ellie right away.
4. Ellie picked Pam up as soon as she saw her.
5. Pam and Ellie walked three hours every day for two months.
6. Ellie had Pam practice carrying a pack for four more months.
7. Pam was afraid and Ellie put her arm around Pam.
8. Ellie and Pam huddled together in the tent.

Unit 2, Lesson 1 • *Pages 77–78*
1. b__a__sic
2. r__a__k__e__
3. f__a__d__e__
4. st__a__ple
5. c__a__n__e__
6. f__a__vor
7. __a__ble
8. b__a__sis
9. t__a__ble
10. g__a__ve
11. f__a__k__e__
12. f__a__de

13. stable
14. case
15. bacon
16. trade
17. table
18. makes
19. apron
20. taste
21. bacon
22. fake
23. date
24. label
25. name
26. rake

Unit 2, Lesson 1 • *Pages 79–80*
1. __i__dol
2. r__i__de
3. __i__tem
4. p__i__pe
5. s__i__de
6. p__i__lot
7. h__i__k__e__
8. __i__ris
Possible Answers: 9–10
9. I sat on the same side of the plane as the pilot.
10. After a long hike in the woods, we went for a ride along the beach.
11. time
12. dime
13. virus
14. kite
15. child
16. silent
17. blind
18. fire
19. wise
20. iron
21. side
22. rise

Unit 2, Lesson 1 • *Pages 81–82*
1. c
2. a
3. e

Copyright © McGraw-Hill Education. Permission is granted to reproduce for classroom use.

Answer Key

4. h
5. f
6. g
7. b
8. d
9. cross out *tufts*; write *peaks*
10. correct
11. correct
12. correct
13. They would be small.
14. He is pulling it out.
15. You made it flat.

Unit 2, Lesson 1 • *Pages 83–84*
1. b   3. a
2. a   4. a

Possible Answers: 5–8
5. Both Hilary and Matt have moved recently.
6. I made this inference because Matt thinks about moving, and Hilary mentions having to start a new school, which is likely due to a move.
7. Both Hilary and Matt are angry about their moves.
8. Hilary drags her feet and wants to throw her backpack. Matt wants to break sticks he finds.

Unit 2, Lesson 1 • *Pages 85–86*
Audience: a teacher or other students
Purpose: to inform my audience
Possible Answers:
Topic: basketball
1. **Declarative:** Basketball teams have five players.
2. **Interrogative:** How tall are the basketball hoops?
3. **Imperative:** Ask Mr. Knox if you can play basketball.

4. **Exclamatory:** Basketball is fun!

Unit 2, Lesson 1 • *Pages 87–88*
1. able
2. paper
3. pale
4. bake
5. sale
6. mild
7. pilot
8. kind
9. time
10. ride
11. pale
12. bake
13. ride
14. able
15. mild
16. pilot
17. paper
18. kind
19. sale
20. time

Unit 2, Lesson 1 • *Pages 89–90*
Practice:
1. were tree trunks.
2. float on the water.
3. are very strong.
4. go quickly down the road.
5. took the boat downstream.
Apply:
6. I
7. C
8. I
9. I
10. I
Possible Answers:
11. Orange trees need plenty of water.
12. My family grows a garden.
13. We like to grow green peppers.

14. We put a flower in our yard.

Unit 2, Lesson 2 • *Pages 91–92*
1. so
2. rose
3. dome
4. wove
5. most
6. joke
7. nose, rose
8. Most, host
9. no, so
10. joke, poke
11. bone
12. roll
13. sold
14. hole
15. jolt
16. hose
17. sold
18. oval
19. owe
20. pose
21. tone
22. old

Unit 2, Lesson 2 • *Pages 93–94*
1. fumes
2. cute
3. United
4. refuse
5. menu
6. music
7. cube
8. fuse
Possible Answers: 9–14
9. That puppy is cute.
10. It will be humid all week.
11. My teacher said I am a good pupil.
12. They used a mule to carry the goods.
13. Please mute the TV.
14. My dad plays the bugle.

Copyright © McGraw-Hill Education. Permission is granted to reproduce for classroom use.

Answer Key

Unit 2, Lesson 2 • *Pages 95-96*
1. down
2. deep hole
3. yes
4. ice
5. yes
6. yes

Possible Answers: 7–10
7. A crevasse happens when a glacier cracks.
8. Fjords are made when glaciers move over the land and scratch it.
9. The speaker does not have much money.
10. The speaker is saying the joke is very old.

Unit 2, Lesson 2 • *Pages 97-98*
1. b
2. a

Possible Answers: 3–8
3. In the summer, I can go swimming.
4. In the summer, my family goes on vacation.
5. Glaciers change Earth's surface.
6. They make fjords.
7. They grind rocks into powder.
8. They move rocks.

Unit 2, Lesson 2 • *Pages 99–100*
Audience: a teacher or other students
Purpose: to inform my audience
Practice:
1. ~~Today, an ounce of silver is worth about sixteen dollars.~~
2. ~~Some wasps build their nests out of mud, while others use chewed-up wood.~~

Unit 2, Lesson 2 • *Pages 101–102*
1. most
2. over
3. nose
4. joke
5. vote
6. menu
7. unit
8. cube
9. fuse
10. mule
11. vote
12. most
13. nose
14. joke
15. over
16. menu
17. mule
18. cube
19. fuse
20. unit

Unit 2, Lesson 2 • *Pages 103–104*
Practice:
1. imperative
2. interrogative
3. declarative
4. exclamatory
5. interrogative
6. declarative
7. imperative
8. exclamatory

Apply:
Possible Answers:
9. I love this cereal!
10. What is your name?
11. My family goes camping each summer.
12. Take this note to Mr. Williams.
13. That's fantastic!
14. Could you grab a pencil for me?
15. I ate lunch at 12:30.
16. Give me that pencil.

Unit 2, Lesson 3 • *Pages 105–106*
1. blaze
2. music
3. robot
4. bite
5. pilot
6. fume
7. major
8. stroke
9. safer
10. mildest
11. whitest
12. older
13. unit
14. wild
15. blade
16. cuter
17. zone
18. post
19. cradle
20. boldest
21. hive
22. confuse

Unit 2, Lesson 3 • *Pages 107–108*
1. knob
2. gnarl
3. wrinkle
4. design
5. knife
6. wrench
7. knot
8. align
9. knelt
10. wrong
11. gnat
12. wreck
13. wrap
14. knack

Unit 2, Lesson 3 • *Pages 109–110*
1. a
2. a
3. a

Copyright © McGraw-Hill Education. Permission is granted to reproduce for classroom use.

Answer Key

4. b
5. lofty
6. restless
7. settler
8. shivery
9. restful
10. security

Unit 2, Lesson 3 •
Pages 111–112
Possible Answers: 1–6
1. orange (underlined)
2. round (circled)
3. medium (underlined)
4. blue (underlined)
5. round (circled)
6. tiny (underlined)
7. Both texts say a person should kneel under a strong table.
8. *Text 2* says that it is safer to stay put during an earthquake because falling items such as a lamp are more likely to hurt a person than anything else. *Text 1* does not give reasons for the steps it describes.

Unit 2, Lesson 3 •
Pages 113–114
Audience: a teacher or other students
Purpose: to inform my audience
Practice:
Masked crabs are animals that use seaweed for protection. The crabs first tear the seaweed until it is soft. ~~Seaweed is a type of water plant~~. Then the crabs put the seaweed on their bodies.

Masked crabs live in the North Atlantic, North Sea, and Mediterranean Sea. ~~The Mediterranean Sea is big.~~ Masked crabs walk backward to burrow in the sand. The crabs use their antennae to make a breathing tube.

The crabs have reddish brown and yellow colors. ~~Blue is my favorite color.~~ The crabs normally are about four centimeters long. The males are twice as big as the females. The crabs have four teeth. Two of their teeth are between their eyes.

Masked crabs like to eat worms and mollusks. These creatures are found where it is sandy. ~~You can find dead masked crabs on the beach.~~

Unit 2, Lesson 3 •
Pages 115–116
1. knot
2. knife
3. gnat
4. sign
5. wren
6. write
7. sharper
8. longer
9. fastest
10. thickest
11. fastest
12. sharper
13. thickest
14. longer
15. gnat
16. write
17. knife
18. wren
19. sign
20. correct

Unit 2, Lesson 3 •
Pages 117–118
Practice:
1. John **A**dams and John **Q**. **A**dams were presidents of the **U**nited **S**tates of **A**merica.
2. If the president of the **U**nited **S**tates is a man, then he is called **M**r. **P**resident.
3. Presidents **T**. **R**oosevelt and Franklin **D**. **R**oosevelt were cousins.

Apply:
4. Where does snow come from?
5. Icy droplets of water in clouds turn into snowflakes.
6. It is amazing that no two snowflakes are alike!
7. Where do the water droplets come from?
8. The BrownCow milk is the brand my mom buys.
9. I brought my shirt from FashionFabulous.
10. I bought a bag of FreshestFine oranges.
The architect **I**. **M**. **P**ei was born in **C**hina in 1917. **M**r. **P**ei has designed many large, beautiful buildings. In the 1960s, he designed the terminal at **JFK I**nternational **A**irport in **N**ew **Y**ork. A landscape architect designs gardens and outdoor spaces. The first person to call himself a landscape architect was **F**. **L**. **O**lmsted.

Copyright © McGraw-Hill Education. Permission is granted to reproduce for classroom use.

Answer Key

Copyright © McGraw-Hill Education. Permission is granted to reproduce for classroom use.

Unit 2, Lesson 4 •
Pages 119–120
1. complete, e_e
2. secret, e
3. began, He
4. She, compete
5. fever
6. athlete
7. pretest
8. These
9. concrete
10. be
11. compete
12. Beware
13. remodel
14. theme

Unit 2, Lesson 4 •
Pages 121–122
1. pride
2. maple
3. robe
4. find
5. accuse
6. brave
7. tempo
8. delete
9. size
10. bacon
11. stampede
12. menu
13. total
14. trade
15. child
16. amuse
17. O, i, o
18. u_e
19. i_e
20. a
21. e_e
22. i

Unit 2, Lesson 4 •
Pages 123–124
1. d
2. b
3. a

4. c
5. plates
6. interact
7. boundaries
8. structures
9. collide
10. absorb

Unit 2, Lesson 4 •
Pages 125–126
Possible Answers: 1–5
1. the ground was cracked and dry.
2. lava flowed over the land.
3. the field was filled with plants.
4. there was a flood.
5. the shed fell down.
6. There is an earthquake underwater.
7. People want to be safe from earthquakes and tsunamis.
8. Energy is released in seismic waves.

Possible Answers: 9–10
9. The family learns what to do if an earthquake happens.
10. The family makes sure their house is strong and well-built.

Unit 2, Lesson 4 •
Pages 127–128
Audience: a teacher
Purpose: to inform my audience
Practice:
1. F
2. F
3. I
4. F
5. F
6. I

Unit 2, Lesson 4 •
Pages 129–130
1. begin
2. meter
3. these
4. label
5. gate
6. wild
7. vine
8. bonus
9. spoke
10. use
11. vine
12. spoke
13. gate
14. use
15. wild
16. bonus
17. these
18. meter
19. begin
20. label

Unit 2, Lesson 4 •
Pages 131–132
Practice:
For a **big**, **green** plant
Or a **tiny**, **little** ant
Resting in the **quiet** woods
is **nice**.
For a **tall** oak tree
Or a **busy**, **buzzing** bee
Being in the **bright** sun
is **nice**.
Each **living** thing must
Share **cool** shade and just
Take a **long** break in paradise.
Apply Possible Answers:
1. red   crisp
2. bright   yellow
3. furry   striped
4. warm   hooded
5. green   city
Possible Answers: 6–8
6. The blue sky was beautiful this morning.

Answer Key

7. The confused girl was unsure which way to go.

8. I have a very gentle dog.

Many creatures live in the forest. **Blue** birds and **brown** owls live in the forests. **Red** deer and **gray** squirrels live there too. **Green** frogs live in the forests that are near water. Sometimes a **white** rabbit can be found hopping through the **thick** forest. Have you ever seen a bear in the forest? I saw **two** bears yesterday.

Unit 2, Lesson 5 •
Pages 133–134

1–2 *ea:* dream, cheat
3–4 *ee:* week, feet
5. week
6. dream
7. cheat
8. feet
9. creak
10. passed
11. fined
12. reel
13. hear
14. need
15. lead, /ē/
16. wind, /ī/
17. lead, /e/
18. wind, /i/

Unit 2, Lesson 5 •
Pages 135–136

1. beagle
2. between
3. legal
4. seaweed
5. delete
6. complete
7. resubmit
8. extreme

9. reheat
10. depend
11. treat, she, prefer, peanuts, sweet
12. weeks, bean, zebra, speak, seems

Unit 2, Lesson 5 •
Pages 137–138

1. mist, haze
2. plowed
3. blurry
4. grazed
5. settlers
6. b
7. b
8. a
9. a
10. b
11. b
12. a

Unit 2, Lesson 5 •
Pages 139–140

1. first
Possible Answers: 2–4
2. Next
3. Next
4. Then
5. Finally
6. Dinosaurs grazing
7. Ice everywhere
8. Settlers and wagon
9. Farm 100 years ago
Possible Answer: 10
10. Next the speaker would go down to breakfast and tell the mother all about the strange thing that happened.

Unit 2, Lesson 5 •
Pages 141–142

Audience: a teacher or other students

Purpose: to inform my audience
Possible Answers:
Topic: Aunt Rita
- a photograph of Aunt Rita
- a map of Yugoslavia
- a photograph of a VA hospital
- a drawing of Aunt Rita pushing a soldier in a wheelchair

Unit 2, Lesson 5 •
Pages 143–144

1. we
2. eve
3. sleep
4. steel
5. creek
6. knee
7. reel
8. steal
9. creak
10. real
11. The water in the <u>creek</u> rose rapidly after it rained.
The rusty swing let out a loud <u>creak</u> as Sam sat down.
12. My dad bought me a new fishing <u>reel</u>.
These are <u>real</u> flowers, not plastic ones.
13. The thief was caught red-handed trying to <u>steal</u> the diamonds.
An ocean liner is made of <u>steel</u>, but it still floats.
14. sleep
15. reel   real
16. we   knee
17. eve
18. creek   creak

Answer Key

Unit 2, Lesson 5 •
Pages 145–146
Practice:
1. axes
2. rockets
3. skies
4. wishes
5. geese
6. hooves
7. babies
8. people

Apply:
9. **Plural:** trees, environments
10. **Plural:** Fungi, trees
11. **Plural:** Branches, leaves
12. **Singular:** stem, tree, trunk
13. **Singular:** meadow; **Plural:** Geese, sheep
14. **Singular:** fish, aquarium **Plural:** fish
15. **Singular:** Jake, soccer **Plural:** feet
16. **Singular:** flower
17. There were many men in the meeting.
18. A team of oxen plowed the field.
19. The children were ready for recess.
20. I think our house might have mice.

Unit 2, Lesson 6 •
Pages 149–150
1. bulge
2. destructive
3. catastrophes
4. majestic
5. swelling
6. seep

Possible Answers: 7–12
7. magma rises underground.
8. called creative eruptions.
9. hot gases.

10. streams down the sides.
11. seep out of them.
12. a rounded dome.

Unit 2, Lesson 6 •
Pages 151–152
1. Volcanoes exist on other planets.
2. There are several ways to classify volcanoes.
3. The volcanic rock pumice has many uses.
4. Volcanoes have many shapes.

Possible Answers: 5–18
5. Volcanoes are creative.
6. Volcanoes can happen in surprising places.
7. Volcanoes can suddenly erupt and destroy mountains. Earthquakes can cause floods that wash away trees.
8. Glaciers can slowly move across the land and change it. Lava from underwater volcanoes can slowly make new islands.

Unit 3, Lesson 1 •
Pages 153–154
1–4 *ai_:* aim, paint, rain, waist
5–8 *_ay:* okay, display, away, maybe
9. holiday
10. braid
11. explain
12. bait
13. drain
14. wait
15. away
16. Maybe
17. sway
18. Spray

Unit 3, Lesson 1 •
Pages 155–156
1. tame
2. gray
3. pair
4. hay
5. sale
6. name
7. train
8. play
9. wave
10. chair
11. a. rake
12. c. rain
13. b. clay
14. d. gate
15. a. grapes
16. d. tail
17. c. May
18. b. pair
19. c. skate
20. a. inflate

Unit 3, Lesson 1 •
Pages 157–158
1. plant
2. flee
3. flexible
4. waste
5. expired
6. vital
7. install
8. expired
9. landfill
10. ensure
11. clogged
12. vital

Unit 3, Lesson 1 •
Pages 159–160
1. c
2. b
3. b
4. a

Possible Answers: 5–10
5. dental hygenist; their hands are in people's mouths.

Copyright © McGraw-Hill Education. Permission is granted to reproduce for classroom use.

Answer Key

6. nurse; they deal with blood.
7. cleaning a classroom
8. emptying the trash
9. install new pipes
10. fix clogged pipes

Unit 3, Lesson 1 •
Pages 161–162
Audience: a teacher or other students
Purpose: to entertain
Prewriting Possible Answers:
- a boy and a girl chasing a dog across a field
- a boy with a worried look on his face sitting high up in a tree
- two girls on a beach pointing down the shoreline at a ship washed up on the beach
- a boy running toward a house, with the sky filled with dark clouds and lightning

Unit 3, Lesson 1 •
Pages 163–164
1. rain
2. chain
3. paid
4. stay
5. May
6. play
7. April
8. fable
9. base
10. trace
11. play
12. fable
13. paid
14. base
15. chain
16. May
17. April

18. rain
19. play
20. chain

Unit 3, Lesson 1 •
Pages 165–166
Practice:
1. no
2. yes
3. yes
4. no
Apply:
5. "Let's place a sign-up sheet in the classroom," said Olivia.
6. Mr. Rickerts said, "I'll offer extra credit to anyone who helps."
7. "The weather should be perfect on Saturday," said Luis.
8. "The park will look so much better!" said Olivia.
9. Ethan asked, "What is the sign-up sheet for?"
10. "We are looking for volunteers to help clean the park," said Mr. Rickerts.
Possible Answers:
"What is your favorite food?" I asked.
"I love strawberries and bananas," answered Milo.
"My favorite food is olives," I said.
"I don't like olives at all!" exclaimed Milo.

Unit 3, Lesson 2 •
Pages 167–168
1. shield
2. alley
3. pretty
4. many
5. valley
6. grief

7. y
8. ie
9. ey
10. ie
11. y
12. ey
13. thief
14. empty
15. monkey
16. field
17. money
18. lucky
19. baby
20. honey
21. berries
22. story

Unit 3, Lesson 2 •
Pages 169–170
1. field, _ie_
2. even, e
3. breeze, ee
4. crazy, _y
5. reach, ea
6. trolley, _ey
7. delete, e_e
8. reef/free, ee
9. ponies, _ie_
10. easy, ea, _y
11. refund
12. finally
13. reason
14. chief
15. screen
16. finally
17. chief
18. reason
19. screen
20. refund

Unit 3, Lesson 2 •
Pages 171–172
1. a
2. c
3. b
4. d
5. e

Copyright © McGraw-Hill Education. Permission is granted to reproduce for classroom use.

Answer Key

6. h
7. g
8. f
9. relies
10. role
11. courteous
12. discover
13. true
14. gain

Unit 3, Lesson 2 •
Pages 173–174

1. b
2. a
3. a
4. a

Possible Answers: 5–8

5. A role you have in school is being a classmate.
6. Your role in your family changes as you get older.
7. They need people like plumbers and pest control specialists to fix problems in their homes.
8. They depend on friends and family for support and love.

Unit 3, Lesson 2 •
Pages 175–176

Audience: a teacher or other students
Purpose: to entertain
Prewriting Possible Answers:
Beginning (problem)
• Izzy and dad are outside
• Izzy scared of bat
Middle (events)
• Izzy yells and grabs dad
• He explains bats are good.
End (how the problem is solved)
• Izzy no longer afraid

Unit 3, Lesson 2 •
Pages 177–178

1. field
2. brief
3. lady
4. baby
5. money
6. monkey
7. breeze
8. speech
9. stream
10. teach
11. stream
12. monkey
13. teach
14. money
15. baby
16. lady
17. brief
18. breeze
19. field
20. speech

Unit 3, Lesson 2 •
Pages 179–180

Practice:

1. Henry is **taller** than John, but Max is **the tallest.**
2. **The quickest** way to travel is by flying.
3. **The** play is tomorrow.
4. My mom's flowers are **the prettiest** in **the** neighborhood.
5. A full moon is **brighter** than **a** quarter moon.

Apply:

6. luckiest
7. highest
8. louder
9. faster
10. happier
11. slowest
12. loveliest
13. smaller
14. earliest

Unit 3, Lesson 3 •
Pages 181–182

Possible answers for third answer in items 1–10.

1. leap, ea, peach
2. respond, e, he
3. raise, ai_, plain
4. play, _ay, day
5. athlete, e_e, these
6. major, a, April
7. flake, a_e, bake
8. bunnies, _ie_, puppies
9. jersey, _ey, key
10. sweet, ee, feet
11. squeaky
12. referee
13. shield
14. detail
15. daydream
16. prepare
17. played—made
18. repeat—delete
19. lazy—daisy
20. peeled—yield
21. turkey—quirky
22. meter—cheater

Unit 3, Lesson 3 •
Pages 183–184

1. photo
2. limb
3. comb
4. graph
5. numb
6. phase
7. debt: b
8. hour: h
9. science: c
10. character: h
11. wrestle: w, t
12. adjust: d
13. phone
14. scent
15. listen
16. plumber
17. columns
18. alphabet

Copyright © McGraw-Hill Education. Permission is granted to reproduce for classroom use.

Answer Key

19. island
20. thumb
21. metaphor
22. climbs

Unit 3, Lesson 3 •
Pages 185–186
1. Correct
2. Incorrect
3. Correct
4. Correct
5. while
6. cemented
7. insulated
8. frame

Unit 3, Lesson 3 •
Pages 187–188
1. Fact
2. Opinion
3. Opinion
4. Fact
5. Opinion
6. Fact
7. Opinion
8. Fact
9. Opinion
Possible Answers: 10–12
10. Victor's family went to the opening ceremony.
11. A reporter interviewed Victor.
12. Victor's opinion was that it was exciting.

Unit 3, Lesson 3 •
Pages 189–190
Audience: a teacher or other students
Purpose: to entertain
Practice Possible Answers:
2. A beautiful red cardinal swooped over the pine tree.
3. Ms. White nervously steered her nephew's fancy sports car through the crowded parking lot.

4. Emily dove into the cool, refreshing water of the YMCA's pool.

Unit 3, Lesson 3 •
Pages 191–192
1. phone
2. graph
3. phase
4. limb
5. lamb
6. comb
7. doubt
8. herb
9. half
10. scent
11. scent
12. lamb
13. phone
14. comb
15. correct
16. herb
17. limb
18. graph
19. correct
20. correct

Unit 3, Lesson 3 •
Pages 193–194
Practice:
1. Tuesday
2. New Year's Day
3. December
4. Thursday
5. The Fourth of July *or* Independence Day
6. Saturday
Apply:
Thirty days has september, april, june, and november; All the rest have thirty-one. february has twenty-eight alone; save in leap year, at which time, february's days are twenty-nine.

My class was studying unusual names of cities in the united states. I began my report on february 28, 2015. I read about boulder, colorado. I wonder if the rocks in that city are bigger than the rocks in little rock, arkansas. Do buffaloes really live in buffalo, new york? Does everyone sew in needles, california? I finished my report on march 6, 2015.

The rappahannock river is located in virginia. It is the longest free-flowing river in the eastern united states. It is also a tidal river. The blue ridge moutains are to the west of it. It enters the chesapeake bay, south of the potomac river. The chesapeake bay is near the atlantic ocean. The river goes through fredericksburg, virginia, an important historical city.

Unit 3, Lesson 4 •
Pages 195–196
1. ice
2. policy
3. pencil
4. center
5. lacy
6. city
7. trace
8. civil
9. circus
10. fancy
11. fleece
12. rice
13. circle, slices
14. niece, science

Copyright © McGraw-Hill Education. Permission is granted to reproduce for classroom use.

Answer Key

15. city, space
16. concentrate, excited

Unit 3, Lesson 4 •
Pages 197–198
1. rage
2. logic
3. giant
4. gentle
5. cringe
6. giraffe
7. orange
8. general
9–11 *ge:* digest, twinge, general
12–14 *gi_:* frigid, tragic, ginger
15. message
16. engine
17. digits
18. imagine
19. cottage
20. gentle
21. fragile
22. vegetable
23. large
24. register

Unit 3, Lesson 4 •
Pages 199–200
1. h   5. d
2. b   6. f
3. e   7. a
4. c   8. g
9. progress
10. values
11. revealing
12. blared
13. features
14. sources
15. result

Unit 3, Lesson 4 •
Pages 201–202
1. Compare; both
2. Compare; both
3. Contrast; but
4. Contrast; but

Possible Answers: 5–8
5. The old building did not have cafeteria, but the new building does.
6. The new building has playground equipment, which the old building did not have.
7. The old building did not have room for a garden, but the new one does.
8. The new building has plenty of room for students, while the old one was overcrowded.

Unit 3, Lesson 4 •
Pages 203–204
Audience: a teacher or other students
Purpose: to entertain
Prewriting: Possible Answers:
Beginning (problem)
• Lily caught in rain
• need barrette for hair
• barrette is lost
Middle (events)
• Lily sees door in tree
• shrinks to gnome size
• gnome invites her for tea
End (how the problem is solved)
• gnome gives her barrette
• she becomes normal sized
• she uses barrette

Unit 3, Lesson 4 •
Pages 205–206
1. peace
2. ice
3. face
4. pencil
5. circus
6. spicy
7. age

8. gem
9. large
10. magic
11. pencil
12. peace
13. ice
14. age
15. magic
16. circus
17. face
18. spicy
19. large
20. gem

Unit 3, Lesson 4 •
Pages 207–208
Practice:
1. Fleas, flies, and bees drive me crazy!
2. Insects eat some of the following things: wood, paper, and even other insects.
3. Bats, birds, and reptiles also eat insects.
4. At 10:30 every morning, I eat a red, juicy, and tasty apple.
5. Cars can be red, blue, black, or green.
6. These are the colors on the Italian flag: red, white, and green.
Apply Possible Answers:
7. strawberries
8. bananas
9. blueberries
10. cats
11. dogs
12. birds
13. My favorite foods are strawberries, bananas, and blueberries.
14. My favorite pets are cats, dogs, and birds.

Copyright © McGraw-Hill Education. Permission is granted to reproduce for classroom use.

Answer Key

Flowers have soft petals, pretty colors, and a nice smell. To grow flowers, you must plant the seeds, water the plants, and pull the weeds. Flowers look pretty in a garden, in your office, or in your house. Today we will plant purple pansies, white daisies, and lilies all around the border of the garden.

Unit 3, Lesson 5 •
Pages 209–210
1. sky, _y
2. fried, _ie
3. tight, _igh
4. spies, _ie
5. style, _y

Possible Answers: 6–8
6. My grandma makes the best fried chicken.
7. I could stare at the clouds in the sky all day.
8. These shoes are getting to be too tight.
9. might
10. Why
11. bright
12. applied
13. lie
14. type
15. try—**c.** dry/**a.** high
16. night—**b.** fight
17. sighs—**d.** dries
18. pie—**c.** dry/**a.** high

Unit 3, Lesson 5 •
Pages 211–212
1. idea
2. criticize
3. flies
4. title
5. light

6. incline
7. China
8. shy

Possible Answers: 9–14
9. pride
10. find
11. wild
12. fright
13. pie
14. my
15. quiet
16. prize
17. high
18. diet
19. Why
20. advice
21. unties
22. beside
23. trial
24. shiny

Unit 3, Lesson 5 •
Pages 213–214
1. wilted
2. indeed
3. simmer
4. surely
5. plaza
6. well
7. wilted
8. seasoning
9. gasp
10. well
11. indeed
12. sighed
13. surely
14. wringing

Unit 3, Lesson 5 •
Pages 215–216
1. b
2. a
3. a
4. b

Possible Answers: 5–8
5. The stranger was a traveler.

6. I used the information about a walking stick and a cape, and the fact that he was walking down a road from outside the village.
7. Isabel's mother was not feeling friendly toward the stranger.
8. I used the information about the way she kept the door nearly shut and the rude way in which she addressed him.

Unit 3, Lesson 5 •
Pages 217–218
Practice Possible Answers:
1. Troy and his furry dog went for an exciting walk today.
2. In the middle of the walk, something incredible happened.
3. Troy's dog Buster talked very loudly.
4. Buster told Troy about a secret field where there was a spaceship.
5. Buster and Troy raced to the field.
6. They were playing on the spaceship when the spaceship roared into the sky.

Apply Possible Answers:
crinkly   cautiously
enormous   purple
sopping   remembered

Unit 3, Lesson 5 •
Pages 219–220
1. night
2. right
3. fly
4. shy, try

Copyright © McGraw-Hill Education. Permission is granted to reproduce for classroom use.

Skills Practice 1

Answer Key **R29**

Answer Key

5. try
6. pie
7. lie
8. child
9. pile
10. mice
11. pie   lie
12. shy   try
13. mice
14. night   right
15. pile
16. night
17. child
18. mice
19. pie
20. try

Unit 3, Lesson 5 •

Pages 221–222

Practice:
1. P
2. P
3. S
4. S
5. S
6. P

Apply:
7. are
8. is
9. am
10. have
11. has
12. rakes
13. change
14. have

Unit 3, Lesson 6 •

Pages 225–226

1. i
2. e
3. f
4. j
5. b
6. c
7. a
8. d
9. g
10. h
11. b
12. b
13. a
14. b
15. a

Unit 3, Lesson 6 •

Pages 227–228

Possible Answers: 1–5
1. the family had to end it early.
2. she fell down a lot.
3. it broke.
4. it would not go.
5. he sleeps during the day.
6. Bridge painters are working.
7. The guard hears a noise.
8. Road workers are mending the highway.

Possible Answers: 9–10
9. They buy bagels in the early morning hours.
10. A boat captain eats a sandwich brought by a steward.

Copyright © McGraw-Hill Education. Permission is granted to reproduce for classroom use.